COPING WITH DIFFICULT PEOPLE

CHRISTIAN CARE BOOKS

Wayne E. Oates, Editor

COPING
WITH
DIFFICULT PEOPLE

by

Paul F. Schmidt

THE WESTMINSTER PRESS
Philadelphia

Scripture quotations from the Revised Standard Version of the Bible are copyrighted 1946, 1952, © 1971, 1973 by the Division of Christian Education of the National Council of the Churches of Christ in the U.S.A., and are used by permission.

Book Design by Dorothy Alden Smith

First edition

Published by The Westminster Press ®
Philadelphia, Pennsylvania

PRINTED IN THE UNITED STATES OF AMERICA

9 8 7 6 5 4 3 2 1

Library of Congress Cataloging in Publication Data

Schmidt, Paul F   1947–
  Coping with difficult people.

  (Christian care books ; 6)
  Bibliography: p.
  1. Personality, Disorders of. 2. Pastoral
psychology. I. Title. II. Series.
RC554.S33   616.85′82′024   79–27486
ISBN 0–664–24299–5

To my wife Molly

through whom my cup is filled
with the abiding love of our Father,
the laughter of our children,
the sensitivity to punctuate my German thinking,
and the common sense to guide me along the way

Contents

Acknowledgments

For their thoughtful suggestions, I wish to thank my editorial readers—my brother, the Rev. Richard H. Schmidt; my pastor, the Rev. James L. Collins; and my dear friends Mary Lou Webb and Monica Kehrt. I also appreciate the reliable efficiency and cheerful generosity of my typist, Barbara Landrey. I am especially grateful for the seasoned and practical guidance of my mentor and friend, Dr. Wayne E. Oates.

1. What Is a Character Disorder?

"Watch out for him—he's a real character." "She just has a bad personality." "I can't exactly put a finger on it, but he really bugs me somehow." "She seems to be comfortable with herself, but I find her really hard to be with." "I just can't seem to get close to him—I don't think anybody can." "There's just no feeling there." These are the typical reactions to people whom mental health professionals describe as having "character disorders."

For example, I am working with a young woman who is a chronic liar. She likes to tell stories for the fun of it, and now she has begun to believe some of her own whoppers. Nobody seems to know whether she's being real or not. Also, I have recently seen three young men in therapy who simply refuse to work. They are very successful at playing helpless and no-good, so that others lose patience, fall into playing the good helper, and bail them out every time. The more they get bailed out, the more convinced they are that they *deserve* the best of everything—at others' expense, of course. As in the case of the lying woman, everyone around these people is driven up the wall, and this has been going on for years.

Do you find yourself in a spot like this? Maybe the person

in your life handles pressure by exploding, manipulating, copping out with confusion, going on guilt trips; or by escaping all tension through television, alcohol, work, or some other distracting energy sapper. Maybe you are even wondering if you have a character disorder yourself, if you might be keeping others away from you without knowing it. If you keep having trouble getting along with someone, this book is for you.

FINDING A DEFINITION

What's wrong with these people, and what exactly is a character disorder? Webster's *New Collegiate Dictionary* (1977) defines character as "the complex of mental and ethical traits marking and often individualizing a person," a person's "main or essential nature." Character refers to the personality, the basic traits that are thought to be "characteristic" of a person.

If this definition of character seems vague, understanding and locating the "disorder" can be trickier still. The simple and easy way is just to say that the disorder is *within the characters themselves.* But it is not all that simple. These persons are often fairly stable individuals, and sometimes rather pleased with themselves to boot. The disorder is often more clearly reflected in *the discomfort of persons around them,* and in the conflicting and inconsistent approaches that different people take in trying to get along with these characters.

For the purpose of this book, a good working definition of a character disorder is one that is consistent with both modern psychiatry and basic Christianity. And it must be one that speaks to the average American. The definition I present here relies heavily on the popular psychiatric notion of character style. A *character style* is a person's habitual way of seeing the world, coping with emotions, and relating to people. A *character disorder*, then, is a long-standing character style that meets three criteria. First, it is not accompanied by any of the other major signs of psychiatric disorder—significant distortions in the perception of reality (the person has "gone off his rocker" and "lives in another world"); severe and unmanageable anxiety (has become more jumpy, tense, or nervous in recent months); or signs of disability due to physical damage to the brain or other organs (shows symptoms of a stroke or brain tumor, for example). Second, the character style serves to protect the person from the full experience of emotion and close personal relationships—the person can't get close to others because he or she lacks an accurate sense of inner feelings. Finally, those who do seek to get close and stay close to the person tend to become frustrated, and the harder they try the more confused and uptight they get.

The most significant feature of this definition is that a character disorder is not seen as a deviance in a person's behavior that constitutes a threat to society, nor as a medical disease that can be treated by psychiatric intervention. Rather, it is seen as a person's characteristic style of thinking, feeling, and relating to others, which blocks the person's own emotional growth and prevents the forming of satisfying, close, and stable relationships with others. It differs from other forms of psychiatric disorder in that there are no obvious symptoms of distress or disability. Moreover, people with character disorders often feel good about their character style, even if it bugs others to death. In fact, they usually see their basic character style as a central and very important aspect of who they are, and thus the character disorder is extremely resistant to change. A typical professional therapist would probably tell you that character disorders have a poor chance of improvement with psychotherapy alone. The "treatment of choice" is to teach all those around these "characters" how to love them in a way that works. They need to know how to hold the characters more responsible for their styles of thinking, feeling, and behaving, and for the price they pay in their relationships with other people. Thus in writing this book to the pastors, counselors, friends, and family of people with character disorders, and of course to the characters themselves, I am writing to the very ones who can most effectively work for change in the character styles of these people.

Character Disorders Then and Now

The importance of the church, pastoral counselors, friends, and family is also seen in tracing the growth of the understanding and treatment of character disorders through history. The concept of character runs throughout the wisdom literature of the Bible. Proverbs, for example, speaks repeatedly of persons who by their very nature are lazy, deceitful, quick-tempered, rebellious, sexually immoral, materialistically possessive, gluttonous with food and drink, and too proud even to listen to advice from a friend.

Likewise, the life-style and teachings of Jesus brought a refreshingly clear focus on character and the motives of the heart. The most powerful example is the Sermon on the Mount, in which Jesus taught his followers to look beneath behaviors such as murder, adultery, divorce, legal revenge, and even such righteous, character-decorating behavior as praying, giving alms, and showing kindness to friends. He taught rather that persons can be fairly judged only by their motives, attitudes, and habitual patterns of thinking. Such a viewpoint is the foundation of character analysis, and the Christian has thought in terms of character ever since.

Moreover, Jesus' death and resurrection have enabled Christians to deal with the symptoms of overt sinful acts by finding a spiritual rebirth of character from within. Former Nixon aide Charles Colson shows this in his recent book, *Born Again.* For this reason, until the last century character disorders were dealt with primarily by priests, through confession and acts of penance within the local church. For over a thousand years, the primary "character disorders" were the patterns of values, thinking, and behavior known as the Seven Deadly Sins—pride, envy, anger, greed, apathy, lust, and gluttony. Detailed confessors' manuals based on the Seven Deadly Sins were in use throughout the Middle Ages, and they read much like the handbooks of psychotherapy in use today. These concepts are still alive and well, as evidenced by Henry Fairlee's *The Seven Deadly Sins Today* (1978). Efforts are now being made to validate and publish personality tests measuring just these seven traits (Backus, 1969; Schmidt, Oates, and Backus, 1977; Schmidt, 1980).

The mental health professions also have much to teach us about dealing with character disorders. Sigmund Freud assessed the essential character style through looking at how his patients viewed and reacted to him ("transference analysis"). His disciple Wilhelm Reich studied the ways in which people defend against the experience of strong emotions, calling this process "character analysis." But probably the most helpful book in understanding character styles is David Shapiro's *Neurotic Styles* (1965). In this book, Shapiro describes four major styles of character disorder, combining intellectual clarity and depth with the colorful, earthy touch of a novelist. Our present understanding of character disorders owes much to the way he relates disorders of thought, mood, and interpersonal relationships to typical character styles.

The American Psychiatric Association has recently revised its diagnostic manual (*Diagnostic and Statistical Manual of Mental Disorders* III), placing new emphases on the concepts of habitual life-style, the impact of personality traits on others, and the resistance to change encountered in these people. In fact, this new manual now requires psychiatrists to evaluate the character style of *all* patients, and to include this assessment in all psychiatric diagnoses to help predict what kinds of symptoms will develop under increased stress.

Are These People Sick or Crazy or What?

These manuals for psychiatric diagnosis are the central resources used by mental health professionals who think of a character disorder as a mental illness. When Freud pioneered a medical approach to treating disturbed people, it was a welcome change from the harsh, punitive approach of the Victorian age, which treated these people as hopeless sinners who should be isolated and punished. Guilt-ridden people who were vainly trying to will their symptoms away found a safe environment in which to explore and confess forbidden thoughts and impulses. The more recent discoveries about brain chemistry and psychiatric drugs have greatly advanced the acceptance of the medical model.

As helpful as the idea of mental illness has been, we push it too far when we try to understand character disorders as basic sicknesses. Illness implies a physical cause and a cure, neither of which has been found for these disorders. Also, the role of patient allows the character to leave the responsibility for cure to the doctor, the pill, or the hospital experience, but none of these have been very effective, especially when the character expects them to do all the work.

We are seeing in our society today evidence of the decline of the medical view of character disorders. Homosexuals, still diagnosed in the same category as the personality disorders, are strongly protesting being labeled as mentally ill. They are saying that many of their number do what they do by choice and not by compulsion. Similarly, some alcoholics and criminals have not responded successfully to psychiatric, illness-oriented treatment programs that assume erroneously that all these people want to change but just don't know how. By telling them that they are sick and unable to change without "treatment," we may be deeply insulting them and reinforcing their refusal to change. What we overlook is that though we may despise their behavior, a major part of them sees the same behavior as essential to their well-being. They aren't "hurting" like anxious neurotics—they hurt us. It is not that they can't change—sometimes they don't really want to change. So why call them mentally ill?

How About Sin?

The move away from calling these people sick has been cheerfully noted by the director of the Menninger Foundation and past president of the American Psychiatric Association, Dr. Karl Menninger. In his book, *Whatever Became of Sin?* (1973), he assails church people for allowing what used to be called sin to be redescribed as crime, mental illness, or collective irresponsibility ("it's a sick society"). The concept of sin respects the sinner by holding him responsible. And though sin is bad, every Christian knows that the news about the forgiveness and cleansing of sin is good.

When I speak about character disorders, I am talking about persons who most of all need the help of concerned family and friends in the larger family of the church. These characters have carefully built and guarded some well-fortified walls, and they hide behind these walls from God, from their fellow human beings, and even from themselves. Seen psychologically, they are chiefly unable to give and receive genuine love. Spiritually, they are not living by Jesus' two great commandments to love God above all, and to love others as themselves. This book aims to encourage a *wise* love and respect for these extremely unlovable and unrespectable people. I mean wise love—I do not mean sentimental, unwise love. And I mean the kind of respect that doesn't look down on these people, but that causes one to treat them as fellow human beings trying just like us to make it in this life.

To be able to love and respect people whose characters are out of order with ours, we must first understand them. Seeing them as cruel, pitiful, or weird will only help us keep our distance from them. In succeeding chapters, I want to explore some of the more common and interesting styles of character disorder. Each chapter will present a thorough and lively picture of the particular character style, and will look at ways of offering to those persons a more honest, intimate, liberating, and loving relationship.

Before I describe the particular styles, you may wish a more thorough understanding of how the character style is formed and how it grows and changes. I will discuss these matters in the following chapter, which will be somewhat more abstract and academic than the ones that follow. In it, I will show how the growth and change process affects moral reasoning and predominant character traits. I will give general suggestions on how to encourage growth and change in another person's basic character style.

2. The Genesis and Exodus of Character Disorders

How They Come and How They Go

Character styles develop in stages. With each succeeding phase of growth, one deals with a new set of conflicts. One's styles of learning to cope with these conflicts also change. So if you're interested in offering a person a chance to change his or her style, you won't know the best approach unless you know which stage of growth the person happens to be in at the time.

In this chapter, we will look at the typical stages of development from two points of view—styles of moral reasoning and predominant character traits. These stages of development will seem much more real once you get to know a woman I will call Janet Green. In the year that I worked with her off and on in counseling, the roots of her character style became apparent. When she set about to change her style, the process of change was difficult and quite interesting.

THE CASE OF JANET

Janet was a social worker about thirty years old. When she came to me she was hoping to break a chain of several love affairs she had carried on behind her husband's back. Her last affair had been with her husband's best friend. She was beginning to feel guilty over the affairs, over falling out of love with her husband, and especially over the effect the affairs were having on their three school-age children, whom she dearly loved. Now she was about to fall for a man in her own church, and she sensed that it would be nearly impossible to hide it if she did. But oh how she loved the challenge of playing Jekyll and Hyde!

I thought of Janet as a soap-opera character. Her life-style was to indulge herself and then deceive others, supposedly to keep from hurting them. She was beginning to want others' approval, but she sought this by splitting herself up and playing different roles for different people. She had learned to enjoy wearing masks, and to describe life as one big soap opera.

An only child who wasn't particularly wanted by her parents, Janet was alone a lot during adolescence. One or both of her parents were always working the night shift and leaving her unsupervised. She learned from them how to keep her social life completely separate from those she loved. Her parents never mentioned to each other what they did after work, but they would hint to Janet how they were cheating on each other. So she started doing the same thing, adding to the fun of sleeping with older boys by not telling anyone about it. The cover-up got to be as much fun as the affairs themselves.

Things became interesting when she seduced and eventually married a young man enrolled in a seminary. She loved him and fully hoped that his unselfish integrity would rub off on her. Their passion began to die out after their first child, and her husband seemed to become more emotionally involved in church than in his marriage. When she began working nights, she started burning the sexual candle at both ends.

I could sense some guilt in her, because a part of her learned to profess religious beliefs in order to gain acceptance. But this was only one of her roles in the soap opera. Around other sensual people, she seemed powerless to be faithful to her husband.

When Janet came to me for therapy, she was hoping to end her affairs. But she was afraid to share her sexual needs with her husband for fear of hurting him if he couldn't satisfy her. The first stage of therapy was aimed at helping her to identify those needs, and to begin sharing them again with her husband. But she could not work through her fears of hurting him. After nine sessions she broke off treatment and announced that she wouldn't tell him what she was doing. Her basic character style of deceitful indulgence again began to show.

But like so many people who enjoy the thrill of a cover-up, she played it more and more dangerously. She called me back in a panic four months later when her husband walked in on her talking with her lover in a bedroom at a party. I insisted on seeing them as a couple. During the three-hour session she confessed most of her deeds to him and promised to try to be faithful. They identified their unmet needs, and agreed to try sincerely to express and meet their needs in the marriage.

Three months later I learned that she had continued to be unfaithful and he had filed for divorce. A month later she called me in a desperate state. She was living alone for the first time, and she was overwhelmed with guilt for hurting her husband and three children so much. I told her that this kind of hurt and guilt was bound to happen with her deceitful, selfish life-style. I said that I couldn't help her unless she was willing to make a complete change, and come clean with *everybody* in her life about who she really was. But instead of coming in for therapy, she let the divorce go through and moved in with her lover from the church.

Several months later the newness was wearing off with her lover, and seeking another affair seemed ridiculous to her. She called me for an appointment, and this time she was ready to change her character style. In seven sessions she wrote full confessions and apologies to her ex-husband and their children. She told everyone in the church what she had been doing. She asked them to forgive her and help her keep on being honest with everybody. She completely changed her appearance and dress, in order to avoid looking seductive. Finally, she drew up a beautiful set of marriage vows, and told her lover that if he wouldn't agree to these and marry her, she would no longer live with him. He chose to marry her, and this marriage is now working on a more solid foundation. She is firmly committed to honesty and fidelity, and to working out their conflicts as they arise. She is now paying the price for intimacy. She experiences the hurts that her actions cause others, and she asks for their forgiveness and help toward maintaining her inner sense of integrity.

Janet had entered a stage of conflict so intense that she questioned her selfishly deceitful style of relating to feelings and people. As her therapist, I helped her explore alternative character styles. I encouraged her to grow, by accepting her unconditionally for who she was (not what she did). Many of her friends and family could also accept her, even after they had felt the hurt of knowing she had lied to them. Because of their acceptance and understanding, she felt secure enough to adopt a new life-style.

Let us now look beyond Janet Green's case and examine the *stages of growth* that most character styles follow. You can look at two different ways of describing the push of conflict outside the person upon change in his or her inner character. Both viewpoints see growth as occurring in stages that are brought on by a person experiencing conflicting demands. Both angles of vision assume that the stages occur in a set order. The person must pass through one phase before entering the next one. Both viewpoints will suggest strategies for agitating the person's experience of conflict, and for giving him or her the support needed in order to resolve it in a mature and solid way.

THE GROWTH OF MORAL REASONING

Lawrence Kohlberg has described six stages of moral reasoning that persons tend to go through as they mature. These stages of reasoning have nothing to do with what a person believes to be right or wrong—that may or may not change from one stage to the next. What does change is the kinds of reasons they use to make moral decisions. Of course, if persons think about a question of right or wrong with a different type of reasoning, they are very likely to come up with new answers. The new answers may be either more or less moral than the old, but at least they are more mature.

To challenge people's thinking, Kohlberg presents them with moral dilemmas to solve. One of his most famous dilemmas is this: Suppose that you are a man living in Europe, and your wife is dying of a rare disease. A recently developed drug is the only known cure, but in your country the drug is in short supply. The only place to get the drug is a local pharmacy, but the pharamacist there is selling it for a very high price. You can't afford to buy it, much less travel somewhere else to buy it. You have begged the pharmacist to sell it to you at a lower price or on credit, but he firmly refuses to do so. Now what would you do, and why?

Stage 1 for Kohlberg focuses on *punishment and obedience,* so that it is the immediate physical consequences of an action that makes it good or bad, right or wrong. For a baby, only a loving or a spanking right now is likely to change behavior. Whatever authority figures tell one to do is considered right during this stage. A typical stage 1 answer to the dilemma might be: "I wouldn't steal the drug, because the cops would catch me and put me in jail. Besides, I might get hurt breaking the window of the store or the drug cabinet."

Stage 2 is the approach of *instrumental hedonism,* in which what's right is whatever satisfies your needs. "If it feels good, do it." It might be right to give to others as long as you're sure they'll pay you back. It's a you-scratch-my-back-and-I'll-scratch-yours kind of thing, but only if you can scratch my back better than I can. "Well, I wouldn't want to sacrifice my money to take out a loan for the drug, and I wouldn't want to do without a wife to wash my clothes and dishes, so I guess I'd just steal the drug to save her."

Stage 3 is the *"good boy/nice girl"* approach, in which good or right behavior is whatever pleases and helps others, and thus wins their approval. "I guess I'd pray and work real hard to get the money somehow—that way my parents and wife and everybody would be real proud of me. They would *give* me the money I need."

Stage 4 is the familiar *law and order* orientation, in which right behavior is doing your duty, showing respect for authority, and preserving the law and order of society. "Well, I sure wouldn't steal it, because that's against the law. If one person could steal, everybody would start stealing. I guess I'd owe it to my wife to work as hard as I could to get the money for the drug."

Stage 5 is the *morality of contract*—what's right is what preserves individual freedoms without breaking the law. Unlike the previous stage, laws are seen as being changeable to meet human needs, and founded on acceptance by the majority of those under the law. "I would see if the police could make him sell me the drug at a lower price. If that failed, I would steal the drug and try to convince the police and judge that I should not be sent to jail."

Stage 6 is based on *universal principles of conscience,* so that you decide what is right on the basis of some abstract ethical code that considers such matters as justice, equal rights, and respect for each person's dignity and individuality. "To allow my wife to live and pursue happiness, and to do what I would want done unto me if I were the pharmacist or my wife; I would steal the drug and leave a note saying who I was and how I would pay back the debt."

The same level of reasoning could be used to support vastly different behaviors. Consider these other stage 6 answers: "To do the greatest good for the greatest number, I would steal the drug secretly. That way, my wife could stay alive, the drug would not be wasted, and I could stay with her and out of jail." Or, "I would follow Jesus' example of sacrificing myself to save others—I'd borrow the money and work myself to the bone for the rest of my life to pay the money back."

It is interesting that Kohlberg holds out the possibility of a seventh stage and higher levels of reasoning that he cannot understand. It is also interesting that Kohlberg has found great variation in the ages at which persons change from one level of thinking to another—some adolescents are in stage 6, and some adults never get beyond stage 2. Even though the laws of this country are based on stage 5 reasoning, Kohlberg says that only one adult in five ever reaches this stage. For example, Kohlberg says that the tragedy of Watergate resulted from President Nixon and his staff's understanding a stage 5 document (the Constitution) with a stage 4 mentality.

If you want to challenge somebody's character style to grow, one good approach is Kohlberg's method of moral education. This approach is now gaining wide acceptance in schools and correctional programs across America (*Psychology Today,* February 1979). The general idea is to put the person into a dilemma in which old habits of thinking don't offer much of a solution. In the classroom, Kohlberg might dramatically re-create the rare drug dilemma and have persons play the roles of pharmacist, wife, and policeman to their logical conclusions.

Janet Green provides an excellent example to illustrate Kohlberg's stages. Each of her four committed relationships reflected a different level of moral reasoning. In each case, the level of her motivation reflected the level of reasoning she held when she began the relationship. As a rebellious teenager, she began having sex with older men just for the fun of it (stage 2). This was still the primary motivation for the affair when she first came to me. Later, she began studying to be a social worker. Her need to be in a helping profession expressed primarily her need for social approval (stage 3). When she fell in love, getting married was the only decent thing to do. Her commitment to work on the marriage was largely her commitment to the institution of marriage in society (stage 4). Once she became involved in the church, her devotion to God and to her children grew out of a mature expression of her value for individual dignity and freedom (stage 5). When I first saw Janet, her affair and her cover-up expressed the stage 2 morality that characterized her life-style at that time. The foundation of her new marriage, and the way she presented herself in all her roles after that, showed her devotion to a stage 5 morality of honesty and genuine concern for others.

The Growth of Character Traits

Like Lawrence Kohlberg, Erik Erikson is a professor at Harvard University. But where Kohlberg has focused on styles of *thinking* about moral issues, Erikson has woven together his knowledge about people from three broadly different sources —biology, psychology, and sociology. The beauty of his view is the way it fits so neatly into a spiritual perspective. His books have been read more widely in American seminaries than those of any other author in the psychological sciences.

Erikson's view of character growth makes several important assumptions. He believes that character traits grow out of conflict, and that life presents a series of certain basic conflicts that we all must face one at a time. The strengths worked out in one stage or crisis are then put on the line in the next. For example, no sooner do adolescents emerge with a sense of identity than they tend to risk losing that identity in the next conflict of falling deeply in love. Finally, Erikson believes that each progressive stage allows the person to become involved with a wider social circle. Thus the more mature person can handle commitments not only to parents, siblings, and peers, but also to one's spouse, career, children, and religious faith.

The following chart outlines the eight stages of growth commonly known as Erikson's Eight Stages of Man. The stages are named for the basic conflict underlying each period, and the "virtues" are taken from one of his lectures in San Francisco (1964). The typical ages of onset and the primary focus of relationship represent my synthesis of his writings in several volumes.

ERIKSON'S EIGHT STAGES OF MAN

Stage (Conflict)	Typical Age of Onset	Emerging Virtue or Asset	Primary Focus or Relationship
1. Trust vs. Mistrust	0	Hope	Parents/God
2. Autonomy vs. Shame and Doubt	1½	Will	Self
3. Initiative vs. Guilt	2½	Purpose	Siblings
4. Industry vs. Inferiority	6	Competence	School
5. Identity vs. Role Confusion	12	Fidelity	Peer Group
6. Intimacy vs. Isolation	18	Love	Lover/Spouse
7. Generativity vs. Stagnation	25	Care	Children/Career
8. Ego Integrity vs. Despair	50	Wisdom	Universe/God

1. *Trust vs. Mistrust—HOPE.* The first signs that a little baby is showing a basic trust in the world around him are when he eats, sleeps, and relaxes his bowels. But the first major test of this trust comes when the voices and faces of Mommy and Daddy become different from all the others that loom up for a peek, a smell, a kiss, or a snuggle. The baby has been tamed, as the Little Prince would say (Antoine de Saint-Exupéry, *The Little Prince,* 1943). Now, what does Baby do when Mommy and Daddy leave too soon—can the baby let them out of sight without being overwhelmed with fear or anger? To develop a basic trust in Mommy, Daddy, and life itself, Erikson believes that at first the parents must answer the cry for help and comfort *consistently* (not immediately, not perfectly, but consistently). Once the child's needs are met consistently, a basic sense of hope is formed, a trust that the world around the child will be able to satisfy whatever needs may be expressed.

The feeling that life is worth living starts in this stage. When this basic trust is gone, the person begins to long for death. Eating and sleeping may be very difficult. He or she struggles to hold the basic belief that there is some type of God that sustains, guides, and enriches life. The person who has lost this basic trust needs the same kind of unconditional love and caring as a newborn baby, says Erikson. Many people today go into a hospital to find this kind of support. But the better (and much cheaper!) approach is to pull together a supportive group of family and friends to assure the person that his or her life is valuable to them.

2. *Autonomy vs. Shame and Doubt—WILL.* When toilet training begins, children try to learn to control themselves. They learn to "hold on" and "let go," not only at the toilet

but also with their toys, mouth pacifier, and temper. The people around them need to reward their letting go. One danger is to come down so hard for holding on that they are too uptight and insecure to turn loose. If parents can moderate their discipline, then children gain a sense of self-control and willpower. The foundation for self-discipline has begun. They learn a balance between the experiences of limits and liberty, of law and grace. This is also the time when they learn that things are to be used and people are to be loved, not vice versa.

If the threat of punishment is too great, children risk losing the sense of basic trust gained in the previous stage. The more trust one has, the more threat one can stand. If children are overwhelmed by punishment, one danger is shame—they turn their anger against themselves. Instead of trying to figure out and control the world around them, they will turn against themselves all their urge to discriminate and manipulate. This relentless self-consciousness is the infantile version of obsessive-compulsive neurosis, in which the adult forever analyzes thoughts and impulses, trying desperately to keep them in complete control.

"Doubt is the brother of shame," Erikson says. In toilet training, the products of "the unseen behind," which feel so good when produced, are called ugly by others. This gives rise to the doubt of "How can something so wrong feel so right?" The mistrust of the unseen, the world behind, and the privately pleasurable are born in the basic doubt of this stage. In its extreme form, the adult settles into a paranoid mistrust of the unknown, of what's "behind," and of the things that give pleasure. As with shame, the cure for doubt is for caring people to support letting go, and gently to show the person how too much holding on and holding in is not good.

3. *Initiative vs. Guilt—PURPOSE.* Once children have gained enough control of themselves, they naturally turn to explore the world around them. The child is "on the make," taking pleasure in attack and conquest, approaching and charming, acquiring and creating. The dangers here are that the child's active, manipulative efforts will either be unrestrained or else too severely punished. If no limits are set, the habit of "acting out" desires and impulses will be formed. Out of such a permissive environment, Janet Green grew to become quite uninhibited in her pursuit of sexual pleasure.

At the other extreme, children can become so inhibited and guilty that they harshly criticize active, creative urges in themselves and others. The prudish person who condemns all the violence and sex in the world (and denies any part in these things) probably got started in this stage. The sense of guilt that emerges from this period is genuine conscience, felt even when the person is alone and acts in private. It is more mature than the shame of the previous stage, which is merely the fear of being discovered. A healthy balance between initiative and guilt is encouraged by showing a permissive attitude toward exploring activity, balanced with a clear, firm—and once again, consistent—communication of limits. "It's O.K. to throw your ball around, but only in the kitchen or outside."

4. *Industry vs. Inferiority—COMPETENCE.* When school begins, the emphasis is on what children can achieve and produce. They are rewarded for focused, steady, and productive *hard work.* Janet Green's history of academic and professional success grew out of the dedication to hard work that she learned at this stage. The pitfalls of parents in this phase include expecting too much or too little, thereby raising

children who either work themselves to the bone or expect others to do all the work. As with other stages in Erikson's system, this one builds on the character traits acquired in earlier stages. The degree of competence and dedication depends greatly upon how much initiative, autonomy, and trust have emerged from previous stages. What you can do for people stuck in this stage is help them set some *reasonable* goals. Then you not only can express your faith that they can reach them but can make it clear that you *expect* them to accomplish their goals. Your faith and reasonableness will help them get over their depression and fear of failure. If there is still no sign of progress or effort, then you are probably dealing with laziness and passive aggression. The treatment of choice for persons with these attitudes is to light a fire under them. "From now on, your allowance will depend on how much schoolwork you do."

5. *Identity vs. Role Confusion—FIDELITY.* We now enter the stormy seas of adolescence. With all the rapid changes in the hormones, and in the size and appearance of the body, it is an awesome challenge to keep the aggressive and sexual urges in line with the standards of the conscience. The longing for sexual love and the freedom of a car run smack up against rules, poverty, and the unpredictable rejections of adolescent love. With all the new desires, social roles, skills, activities, fads, and groups to choose from, the central task for the adolescent is to fashion a cohesive sense of identity for right now. The questions of "Who am I?" and "What do I want to be?" become overwhelming at this time. Adolescents desperately grab onto groups, gangs, teams, clothing and hair styles, musical stars, and especially steady lovers. Then they hold these out to the world as if to say, Here, *this*

is who I am! How do you like me now? Reactions from peers shift greatly with each new addition to the "image." It was Erikson who coined the term "identity crisis," and with adolescence, this is it!

The danger of this phase is role confusion—the inability to gain a solid, stable sense of identity. Increasingly in America today, this stage lasts on into the twenties with people still unable to answer the question that keeps cropping up from within and without, "Just who *are* you, really?" The experience of identity crisis, the life-style of playing unintegrated roles, beautifully describes the dilemma Janet Green was suffering. In none of her relationships could she freely play all her roles, and so she had not been able to "get herself together."

Whatever can one do to help another person through the troubled waters of identity crisis? What such a person needs is a steady sense of acceptance for who he or she is beneath all the roles, masks, and attachments. Parents and loved ones can provide much security by continually looking beneath the behavior, beliefs, and even feelings. They can sense and respond to that basically lovable and worthwhile person who is trying to make something of his or her life.

But how much difference will this make? If you are one of the many parents now trying to guide adolescent children, you may sense that they are being swept away from you by a mighty flood stream over which you have very little control. As scary as it seems to you, just imagine what it feels like to them! How they emerge from this stage will depend a great deal upon the people with whom they choose to live. The more they are surrounded by persons who are dependable and accepting, the faster they will gain a sense of who they are.

And the more capable they will be of sustaining a commitment to a person or group they join.

6. *Intimacy vs. Isolation—LOVE.* As soon as persons gain a solid sense of who they are, they tend to become deeply involved and risk losing the identity they fought so hard to gain. Intimacy is the ability to fuse your identity with someone else's without fear that you are going to lose something in the process. Young adults risk losing their identity not only in romantic love but also in joining the armed forces, becoming inspired by teachers, and joining religious or political groups. The danger of avoiding such involvement is a creeping sense of isolation, a growing life-style of self-centeredness. An aggressive version of this isolation is observed when these persons attack anyone who offers involvement that would threaten the private, cozy, intimate affairs they are having with themselves.

In addition to isolation, there is the danger of becoming so deeply involved with another person or group that the originally solid sense of self-identity is lost. Such dizzying experiences usually end in sudden separation, and the identity crisis must be faced all over again. This was the dilemma Janet faced when she found herself living alone, having just divorced, and having no firm basis of commitment with her lover.

If you are trying to help people find the courage to seek intimacy, the best thing you can do is to assure them of your willingness to maintain their sense of identity. You can point out the creeping misery of isolation, and the growing beauty of intimacy. Whether your help is accepted is beyond your control. They must make the leap toward intimacy utterly on their own. Whether this leap is successful and leads to genuine love will depend mostly upon the one they embrace.

7. *Generativity vs. Stagnation—CARE.* If one has gained a sense of identity and then has had it enriched by giving some of it away to enter an intimate relationship, one is then ready to face the challenge of sharing with others the love and wisdom found in that relationship. For the man this usually means dedicating himself to becoming productive and creative in his vocation. Increasingly, women are also seeking to give themselves to a career, but most will choose to devote themselves at least initially to child rearing. The danger is to see all that has been gained in previous stages (hope, purpose, competence, identity, productivity, etc.) either dry up for lack of use, or be lost by neglect of the relationships that sustain them. The challenge of this stage is to devote energy and concern to help guide and sustain the next generation. This energy, like the love and identity of previous stages, must be given away if it is to grow. It reminds us of what Jesus said about giving one's life away in order to find it.

The best way to help people through this stage is to help them maintain a proper balance between giving themselves away to future generations and relying on the strength they draw from their own generation. The road to health is keeping up a lively dialogue with the younger generation, without neglecting to share with peers the common struggles to succeed at a career and raising children.

8. *Ego Integrity vs. Despair—WISDOM.* The final chapter of life presents a challenge to face old age and death without giving up. For Erikson, ego integrity brings assurance of continued meaning and order in life, acceptance of the limits of life, and awareness of how the strivings of others can be equally legitimate though vastly different. The creative urge

is slowly transferred from one's own life to the collective, spiritual life of humankind. The danger lies in giving in to the despair that one brief life cannot make much difference, that the existence of one person doesn't matter to God or the universe. This despair can turn to disgust, in which thousands of little gripes add up to fuel a deep spirit of bitterness. There is a renewed importance of answering the religious question about the significance and continuity of life on this earth. (It is not because of their good health that so many elderly people make it to church on Sunday morning!) More than at any other stage, the strength these people draw on comes from within. They must rely on the virtues gained through the crises of earlier stages, and on the strength they find in their religious faith.

As a final note it is well to remember that growth arises out of crisis and challenge. Positive growth toward maturity is the response of faith—faith in oneself, faith in others, faith in the creating, sustaining God who lives both within and without. Negative growth back toward infancy is the response called "shrinking back" by the author of the biblical letter to the Hebrews. We can challenge another person into crisis. Whether that person shrinks back or responds by growing in faith is beyond our control.

3. Styles of Thinking

The people described in this chapter may seem to be more dominated by their feelings than by their thinking styles. The paranoid seems threatened, hostile, and bitter. The obsessive person feels worried and tense most of the time. And the hysteric is typically insecure, lonely, and craves attention, approval, and affection from others. While such feelings are the first thing you notice about these people, you will see that their emotions result from fixed patterns of thinking about themselves and the world around them. More purely emotional character styles are discussed in the next chapter.

These persons do not quickly change their predominant moods and their habits of behavior. Even so, their moods and their actions usually change more easily than their basic patterns of thinking. These cognitive styles are central to their personality, and to get along with them, you must first of all understand and accept their styles of thinking.

PARANOID STYLES

"People are out to get me, but I'm not going to lose control."

The Basic Paranoid. The problem for paranoids is that they are scared of being overwhelmed by their own feelings. They fear that if they let themselves experience anger, sadness, or sexual desire, the result will be disastrous. They are afraid that they will lose control, appear foolish, become vulnerable to being hurt by others, and eventually go crazy. To deal with this fear, they keep their emotions tightly in check with their impressive brain power.

To keep a tight rein on their feelings, paranoids rely on their stock-in-trade—projection. The hallmark of paranoids is the way they project their threatening impulses and feelings out into the world around them. When they sense an unsettling feeling like anger in the air, they "throw the rascal out." They figure, I didn't start this—you did! The threat that started inside them (the unsettling push of their own feelings) is now seen as outside of them.

In its extreme form, projection leads to the paranoid delusions of persecution or grandeur. After projecting all their evil onto others, paranoids who become schizophrenic may see themselves as some Christlike messiah, destined to be persecuted by an evil world. Another common theme is for paranoids to see themselves as brilliant persons having certain valuable ideas which the CIA, the Mafia, or some other group or person is always trying to steal from them.

But these are the psychotics, the textbook cases. Basic garden-variety paranoids grow right in your own family and neighborhood. They don't distort reality by building up elaborate delusions about the world. They just distort the *importance* of what they see in others. One man I worked with was uncanny in the way he could sense the slightest sign of tension or irritation in my expressions. He would then focus on that sign and try to explore at length what was bothering me. When they sense a threat in the air, paranoids start scanning the environment for clues to confirm their suspicions. Once they find a clue, they go right into their game plan of defending against the threat. If it's anger they have projected, they can be harsh and cruel in fighting back. They don't feel any guilt because, in their opinion, they didn't start it. They are just acting in self-defense. If it's sexual impulses they project, then they heap shame on whoever is supposedly seducing them (and thus avoid feeling ashamed of themselves).

What makes this mental style of projection so hard to deal with is that the more you question paranoids, the more threatened they become, and the more rigidly they stick to their guns. When you question the way they see things, you are merely giving them another clue to confirm their suspicions that you are somehow out to get them. The more you try to tear down the walls of projection they have built, the more they sandbag and retreat from you even further.

Typically, paranoids maintain tight control over their bodies, so that even choice of words and small movements are made in a deliberate, calculated way. The more emotional they get, the more they see themselves as threatened by the emotions of others. They begin to see themselves as having a shrinking and tightening control center in the brain. They see their bodies as instruments to be used, and when parts of their bodies show signs of losing control, these parts are seen as alien, rebellious parts of an imperfect machine.

Because the world as they see it can rise up and threaten them at any moment, they keep themselves *constantly* on the alert and on the defensive. Typically they have a lot of trouble doing spontaneous, passive things such as laughing, crying, playing, or enjoying sensual pleasure. Everything they do is planned for a purpose. The interesting thing is that they think everyone else is just like them. They don't understand spontaneity and play, which they see as a facade displayed for effect. So they aren't interested in being close to you or even in enjoying your company, because they think you are like them. They figure that you would somehow try to capitalize on the situation in order to use it for your own benefit.

To get along with paranoids, you must first accept their basic character style as one that is not likely to change. They will continue to be threatened by closeness and spontaneity, even within a trustworthy marriage or friendship. Remember: they are threatened by their own feelings, by losing deliberate control over emotions that undermine their personal law and order. If you know which feelings most threaten a paranoid, try not to provoke those feelings. Your most effective way of getting through is freely to express and enjoy those feelings in yourself, *without* pushing the paranoid to experience the same thing with you. By your *enjoying* your spontaneity (even the relaxing release of anger can be enjoyed), you teach and subtly invite the paranoid to do the same. A dancing, spontaneous spirit is more inviting by example than a direct invitation through words or pressure.

When a paranoid invites you into his or her delusion ("Don't you think Betty is cruel?"), your best response is to stay out of the projection without attacking it. Talk about your own feelings toward the threat. "Oh, sure she hurts my feelings, but that's life. I usually have a lot of fun with Betty, and if I thought she was intentionally cruel, I couldn't enjoy playing bunko or shopping with her anymore." You don't deny the reality of the paranoid's clue, you just don't make such a big deal out of it that you lose sight of all the positive things.

In one sense, paranoids are brave people who act on their beliefs in spite of what others think. Respect and praise them for that. Then you can show them with your life the power of self-fulfilling prophecy. To a large extent others will treat you as you expect them to treat you. With your courage to act on a positive view of the world, you show them with your example how to redirect their strength. You can show them how to project not their threatening feelings but their comforting ones. "I'm nice to Betty, so she's usually nice to me."

The Suspicious Mind. Persons with this particular style live almost entirely in their heads. They are easier to live with than most paranoids because they have some perspective on what they do. They have an idea that the world might not be as mean and cruel as they think it is, but they are usually afraid to act on this idea and find out. They also have enough common sense to see that acting on their paranoia only serves to increase the feelings of threat and estrangement from self and others. So these are the mild cases. Unless you push them for a reason why they aren't more active emotionally or socially, they usually will keep their suspicions to themselves without putting them into words.

Barry Manilow recently wrote and recorded a song that expresses the feeling of persons entrapped by their own suspicions. Theirs is a life without jolts or surprises. It "goes along as it should. It's all very nice but not very good." Their challenge is getting "ready to take a chance again." This is the theme song for the movie *Foul Play,* in which Goldie

Hawn starts out being scared of involvement on all fronts. But she has become lonely in her alienated life-style. She has lots of very good reasons to remain fearful (she isn't paranoid, people are just out to get her). She doesn't know whom to trust, and her problem is that she has not been trusting anybody. So along comes Chevy Chase, whose companionship and sense of humor are enough to draw her out of her shell.

I recommended the movie to an attractive, thirty-year-old single woman I was counseling. I kept thinking of her when I heard the song, because she had been uninvolved in her personal life for ten years. She was dominated by a suspicious mind. She went to see the movie with a girl friend, and a few weeks later invited a man to go and see it with her. It turned out so well that she invited him to go to the beach for a weekend with her and her brother. In her first session after the beach trip, she said that she had decided she was now ready to leave home for the first time, and to strike out to find a fulfilling life for herself. I still like to think of her driving off into the sunset singing along with Manilow.

The Arrogant Accuser. The next two styles of paranoid thinking have usually had their origins in suspicious minds. But then they began to act on their suspicions in a way that only served to confirm them further. Arrogant accusers are chiefly threatened by their severe conscience, which would criticize them violently for feeling such emotions as hatred or lust. Deep in their subconscious they fear that they are evil, and thus face cruel death by the sword of righteousness. Such fear and harsh conscience were typically learned from their parents' attitudes toward evil. The basic approach here is to scare evil away, and if that doesn't work, shame it into submission. When they grow up they can't wait to leave their parents. Once they do, their own evil desires crop up right away. So often they try to control them with the same scare tactics their parents used. When this doesn't work, they usually marry someone who shares their frightening and forbidding conscience, and make a pact to keep evil desires (and thus fear and shame) completely out of the marriage. Evil is projected out of the marriage. When their own evil desires surface once again, the evil is inside the house and projection becomes a little trickier. They can still deal with their own impulses by seeing them "out there" in their spouses. Then each becomes for the other the very force they both were running from when they married—the self-righteous, ever-watchful, shame-on-you, grounded-for-two-weeks, fire-and-brimstone-preaching PARENT. Thus another generation of arrogant accusers is born.

What happens is that the identified bad apples can't stand the accusations. They sense their accuser's own immoral desires and habits, and try to fight fire with fire. They accuse the accuser. But attacking a paranoid head on only makes matters worse. So if you are the spouse or child of an arrogant accuser, what, pray tell, can you do?

Your first step must be to take away the club that is used on you. Get right with your maker and your conscience, so that you don't fear the hell of God's rejection. In order to do that, you must believe that you have God's love and acceptance, now and forever.

Your second step must be to forgive your accuser. Can you forgive one for poisoning your life with constant threats and accusations? Can you accept the continued poisoning of the lives of others in your family? If you can't forgive, then the curses will fall on you all over again. This time the accusing finger will point at your hatred, and once again you'll be tortured by your own conscience.

So to get along, you must abandon the paranoid's concept of a fire-breathing God and make your peace with the God who lives within your own soul. You discover that though God doesn't approve of everything you do, he doesn't punish you for being tempted, and he accepts you as you are. Once you have acknowledged that, you are ready for step three, to go and love your accuser even as God has loved you. Yours is the kind of love that can give and serve without expecting or needing anything in return. When you expect less, your accuser hurts you less. And the hurts that can't be avoided don't kill the love of the suffering Christ.

This may sound as if I'm preaching, but I honestly don't know how else anyone can get along with an arrogant accuser who pretends to dispense the wrath of God. If you discover a better way, please write and tell me about it.

The Relentless Detective. Relentless detectives are kissing cousins to the arrogant accuser. Such persons are like prosecuting attorneys at work outside the courtroom. They go out and track down not only clues but also hard evidence. There's nowhere they won't go to catch you in the wrong. Relentless detectives differ from arrogant accusers because they are often helplessly dependent on the person they are accusing. Rather than play the part of the arrogant and angry parent, they play the part of the scorned lover. They act as if they have been betrayed and reduced to a helplessly sobbing disaster victim with no reason to live. Whereas the arrogant accuser was operating from a position of strength (the old parental role), relentless detectives feel overwhelmed by weakness. Their approach is thus more desperate and pitiful than the accuser's, and some people find it the harder one to live with.

You may find yourself amazed by the lengths they will travel to gather their evidence. I've seen them travel across state lines to catch a husband or wife coming out of a motel room at the crack of dawn. They spare no expense or time. They leave no stone unturned. They actually seem to enjoy the hunt, and why shouldn't they? Feeling impotent most of the time, the search for damaging evidence is their only experience of power and revenge. They enjoy their detective work just as Lt. Columbo does. Slowly they weave a web of facts, fear, and guilt so tightly that the suspected one cannot move without further self-incrimination.

What frustrates these relentless detectives is that the more evidence they compile, the more their loved ones want to get away from the pressure of being investigated. Like the ones who flee the arrogant accuser, their loved ones can stand only so much guilt and pity at watching the detective dissolve into tears. They are running from the pity as much as from the guilt.

Now a word to the detectives themselves. When you make your lovers feel guilty, it just makes them want to run from you all the more. The only thing that can draw them back is for you to stop using your accusations to drain them dry when you are together. You need to find your own source of strength so that they can once again discover ways to enjoy being with you as lover and companion. They won't be able to get over their guilt or lack of respect for you until you show them that you can pick yourself off the floor and hold your head high, even when their unfaithfulness hurts you.

If you find yourself to be the "defendant" in this case, you are probably not searching for therapy unless your secret lover has just kicked you out. You have decided you're so old and unattractive that you had better start paying your dues and working things out at home as a hedge against age inflation. You can start by saying you're sorry. Then explain as best you can which of your feelings you were running from on your escapades, and tell how you intend to deal with these feelings in the future.

OBSESSIVE STYLES

"I can't seem to get this darn thought out of my mind."

The Basic Obsessive (the Worrywart). Like the paranoid, obsessive people are determined to keep their own feelings in check. They don't want their boats rocked with a sexual impulse, a crippling fear, or an aggressive urge. Everything they experience must be deliberate, planned, and under their tight control. Remember that paranoids project their unacceptable impulses onto others, and then criticize them with strict rules and a parental type of conscience. Obsessives have a different way of dealing with their impulses. They beat them down so they aren't even aware of them. What they project is their strict, moralistic, duty-oriented conscience. Others are seen as driving them to keep their noses in a book, to the grindstone, and otherwise out of trouble. The enemy is not "out there" like the paranoid's; obsessives see the enemy as within—their own whims and impulses. What is seen out there is a vague but ever-present sense of duty.

The chief weapon obsessives use against their feelings is to distract themselves with *details*—predictable, orderly, controllable, often picky little details. We call this "obsessive preoccupation." They focus on concrete ideas and memories —things they can see and touch, and thus sort out. They lose the abstract concepts—the meaning of things—because this provokes emotion. Shapiro has compared the situation to an ant crawling around on a Rembrandt painting. He notices each color and stroke of the brush, but he has no idea what it means. He can't see the forest for the trees.

A good example of this type of thinking is the businessman encountered by the Little Prince in Antoine de Saint-Exupéry's story. This man is busy counting stars, recording his counts on paper, and sticking his papers in the bank as proof that he owned the stars. As he explains to the Little Prince: "I am concerned with matters of consequence. There is no time for idle dreaming in my life." Then the Little Prince asks him an abstract question about his activity, and the businessman ends the conversation in typically concrete thinking:

> "Whatever does that mean?"
> "That means that I write the number of my stars on a
> little paper. And then I put this paper in a drawer and
> lock it with a key."
> "And that is all?"
> "That is enough," said the businessman.

Unfortunately, the more uptight obsessives get, the more rigidly they dwell on trivial details. Under stress they find it hard to shift their mental set to step back and see the whole picture. They may see an image in their mind over and over, like their house burning in a towering inferno, or their spouse burning in a passionate embrace with someone else. They ruminate over these awful images whenever they are uptight, but they never know what the image means. Perhaps it means that they are afraid to leave home, that they are becoming terribly estranged from their spouse, or whatever. When these images flash across their mind, they cannot distinguish between what's possible, what's plausible, and what's probable. The possibility seems as awful as the real thing.

Now, given this basic way of thinking, how would you expect obsessives to make decisions? It is a torturous ordeal indeed! First, they try to see it as a simple case of fulfilling a duty or following a rule. If duties or rules conflict, obsessives begin to get tense. Next they will handle the tension by distracting themselves with endless pros and cons to see if there is a clearly logical choice. Have you known people whose pros and cons are always perfectly balanced, and who get stuck forever in indecision? What they lack is direct experience of their gut-level feelings to push them one way or the other. They are lost in analyzing the indicators of what is the right or logical thing to do. It is like a pilot flying an airplane through a fog, who has only the indicators of his instrument panel to guide his course. He has no direct visual contact with the land. What obsessives cannot do is say, "I just *feel* it's right—I believe this is the best thing to do." Lacking a sense of inner conviction or purpose, they are forever trying to find an external "should" to push them one way or the other.

These people are not easy to live with. You have probably tried to break down their obsession by calling these thoughts unreasonable or unhealthy. You may have also tried to get them to express their underlying emotions, to experience their feelings spontaneously. Chances are you haven't had much luck, because you're asking them to change their basic style of coping with stress. Except for teenagers and children over a period of years, that is expecting too much. What you can do is help them make some adjustments in their coping style. Since they resort to obsessive detail under stress, pick a time when they are feeling secure, and don't push too hard. You can help reduce the pressure from outside by showing them how much their sense of duty is a slave driver of their own making. "Who says you have to?" "Who taught you this thought was so repulsive?" "Besides your imagination, what evidence do you have that your boss would be so upset?"

Another approach is to teach them to substitute more appropriate details to dwell on. Perhaps they could try to recall long passages of Scripture verbatim, or go through an extensive prayer list (rosary beads are ideal for just this purpose). If the thought that flashes across the mind's eye is a horrible one, they can learn by practice to imagine a constructive conclusion to the awful scene. For example, a man with a homosexual obsession could imagine confessing his act, and being cleansed and forgiven. One who dwells on tragic death scenes could continue the scene to see the departed soul going to heaven to rejoin old friends and family.

Finally, you can set a good example for obsessives by accepting your own emotions. Invite them spontaneously to run out for a pizza or a movie some night. Show them you can make decisions on the basis of your inner convictions, and encourage them to do the same. You can't overpower their obsessive walls of defense, but freely expressed emotions are contagious. They will eventually draw obsessive people out from behind their safe little routines.

The basic obsessive is easier to live with than some of the more disordered obsessives who may be marching around in your world.

The Malignant Obsession. Obsessive people can be some of the most pleasant, easy-to-get-along-with persons you'll ever meet. I once had an obsessive as a supervisor for psychotherapy, and he seemed as affable and well adjusted as could be. The danger comes when strong negative emotions are pushed down and the obsessive thoughts become bothersome and disgusting. Some of the people I talk with have simply tortured themselves with obsessive thoughts, and these have taken many forms. One person often panics in worry over whether she remembered to flush the toilet. Another woman has become suddenly terrified of germs every time something makes her uptight. Another young person complained of being horrified and disgusted at the recurring thought of stabbing a stranger with a knife. A perfectionist young man would go over and over his day's performance in dread of discovering some small error he had made. Another person was disgusted at the recurring thought of a homosexual act. Many persons become fixated on the thought of going crazy, or on the possibility of death. These are not persons who get along well until their fear is triggered by a situation in their environment (a crowd, a spider, a snake, a height, etc.). Rather, they are people who push down nearly *all* of their spontaneous emotions. Whenever *any* strong emotion begins to surface, they put up their smoke-screen obsession to distract themselves and others from their own feelings. The obsession can be called malignant because it is repulsive, it grows, and it consumes the life-giving emotions within the character.

These people are examples of obsessive characters turned against themselves. They are punishing themselves with their obsession. To deal with such people, you must first wonder why they are punishing themselves. Usually it is just a desire, a fantasy, or an unacceptable wish. Whatever, you will do well to take an accepting, forgiving stance. Encourage obsessives to confess their awful thoughts or deeds to someone. Suggest that they make restitution somehow, except where this would do more harm than good. Sometimes they will want to involve you over and over in their obsessive ruminations. This can get on your nerves in a hurry. The best approach at these times is not to treat the thoughts as awful or disgusting, but rather as pointless and wasteful. You both have better things to do with your time and energy.

The Benign Obsession. Other obsessive styles seem more benign. People don't find them so disgusting. They may even help to bring out certain positive feelings such as joy and hope. The character style of these people is disordered by their repeated history of going back to a bad habit without recognizing the possibility of reverting to that habit. They use some orderly mental ritual to block out awareness of their own impulses. The most common example is the religious fanatic who keeps backsliding into sin without changing his view of himself. One such man had learned to respond to all his anxieties by obsessively quoting Scripture. What was obsessive was the way he would use it primarily when upset by a religious doubt. He would so distract himself that he would neither solve his emotional problem nor even remember what it was that had upset him in the first place. He had a history of repeated breakdowns that occurred when the obsession could no longer hold back the doubt. I have seen others respond to tension by getting lost in psychological analysis. Another man I know seems to turn every personal affront into a moral or political issue. After he gets off the soapbox he doesn't even remember what set him off. The trouble is that he is more and more easily set off because he has allowed his anger to build up.

To the characters themselves, these truly are magnificent obsessions. They wouldn't change them for the world. So to deal with these people, you must encourage them to make their coping styles even more magnificent. I have found best results encouraging religious people to expand their faith. I challenge them with questions of "what if" they experienced a disgusting or frightening emotion. If their history showed repeated problems with a particular act, I might ask how their increasing faith would decrease the desire to drink, or masturbate, or curse. How would they respond to overwhelming sadness or fear? If they refuse to admit the possibility of what has troubled them in the past, I might suggest that their faith may be weak or immature. This usually challenges them to deal with at least the possibility of experiencing moral or emotional distress. If not, it is best to let them be, and to support their hope that the behavior does not recur.

Hysterical Styles

"I don't exactly know—it just *feels* that way."

The Basic Hysteric (the Scatterbrain). Like obsessive people, those with hysterical thinking styles tend to repress unacceptable feelings, just pushing them down out of their awareness. But whereas obsessives tend to repress *all* strong feelings, hysterics have a way of repressing only emotions that conflict with their present mood. They seem unable to experience ambivalence, or "mixed feelings." While obsessives sharpen their mental focus onto certain details of the world around them, hysterics are notoriously illogical and out of focus as they view the world. To them, the world is often experienced as a buzzing, blurry mess, with no details that can be picked out and analyzed.

Hysterics focus their attention on one of their own internal feelings, in much the same way that obsessives focus on one set of details in the outer environment. Obsessives have a hard time looking at a whole field of details to determine the patterns or meaning of the world around them. Likewise, hysterics have a hard time looking at the full spectrum of their emotions in order to arrive at a comprehensive view of the way they feel about things. As a result, their view of the world is thoroughly colored by their feelings of the moment. We often call this "wishful thinking," but the wish can be negative too. Being "mad at the world" or "down about everything in general" are other examples of how things seem to hysterics when they get lost in one of their moods.

As a consequence of this thinking style, the emotions of

hysterical persons tend to be intense, overreactive and short-lived; they are generally described by others as "shallow" or "put-on." Their feelings seem to be somehow false or "affected," as if the person is merely playing a role in some drama. Later, when you ask them about these emotional experiences, they will have a hard time remembering them, saying, "I don't know what came over me."

With this impressionistic style of thinking and feeling, their behavior tends to be dramatic, impulsive, suggestible, and generally engaging or exciting to those around them. In fact, hysterics tend to crave your involvement with them, and they know how to draw it out of you. They can't get enough of what I call the three A's—attention, affection, and approval. For this reason, they tend to be very demanding and dependent on others. These are the people who leave you feeling drained. I let one person drain me dry one hour a week for two months; she kept saying, "You know, you're the first and only person who has ever helped me."

Trying to get along with these people is a real trip. It is a fascinating adventure from peak to valley, from fiery volcano to deep blue sea. If you have hysterical tendencies yourself, God help you! I once saw two hysterical people who had been married for over twenty years. What a disaster their life together had become! Hysterics need the company of persons who live by reason and common sense. Their subjective view of the world is so colored by whatever they are feeling at the moment that they desperately need another person's more stable, objective viewpoint as a balance; the hard part is helping them to see their need for this balance. Now I didn't say they need to have *your view* of things—they just need to balance their view with yours.

One way to help them see their need for your common sense is to wait for a time when they have become exhausted from their frantic pace and excitement. Once in a while even hysterics stop long enough to ask themselves: "What's it all about? Who am I really?" At these times you can ask them to read this section of this book to find out if they see themselves in it. If so, you can suggest that you two practice sharing your impressions with each other before acting impulsively or making important decisions. If they don't find themselves in these pages, agree with them on three mutual friends whom you could ask to read this and give their opinions. Who knows, maybe you're not as objective as you thought!

Another suggestion will keep you from getting drained. The more excited they are about this and that, the less "together" they are as people. At these very times, they demand the most attention, affection, and approval. Yet these are the very times they are least worthy of your three A's, because they aren't really being themselves at that moment. They aren't centered—they are off on an emotional tangent. I suggest that you not give them so much attention for their histrionics. Save it for their quieter, duller moments. They are running from the loneliness of these moments. Step in and love them at these times; this will begin to give them the security they didn't get as children when they learned how to get attention by being hysterical. It is the insecure child in them that you want to care for and encourage, not the many dramatic roles they have learned to play. If you wonder how long it will take them to grow up, it usually takes longer than it would have taken for them to grow up as a child. They have no set of adolescent peers with whom to share their struggles. They have a great deal to unlearn from their hysterical life-style. So growth is slow. If they can once recognize with you their own immaturity and loneliness, they can commit themselves to becoming less hysterical with you. The commitment they need to make is to try to *act* less impulsively, dramatically, and demandingly, and to make decisions based on reflective judgment rather than on their immediate impressions.

The Naive Romantic. One particular expression of the hysterical style that seems most tragic is the naive romantic. A woman was bewildered about how to deal with men. After seventeen years of a marriage she thought had been ideal, her husband left her suddenly and married another woman, without even waiting for a divorce. Still not believing the whole thing, she kept begging him to come back. When he finally filed to divorce her, she told him she would give him one year to see what he had done and come back. He laughed and told her to forget it, but she and her two daughters waited throughout the year. When the divorce was final, she started repeating her mistakes with other men. Five times she fell romantically in love, only to discover that the men only wanted to use her for her body or her money (she often paid for their dates and bought them presents). After love affair number five she sought therapy, wondering if perhaps she had trouble understanding men. It became apparent that her view of these men had been so colored by her attraction to them that she had been repeatedly blinded to their faults. The extent of her romantic idealism did not surface until our third session, when she brought me several poems she had written. One long poem chronicled the history of her relationship with her ex-husband, whom she described with flowery praise.

She included a couple of other poems, all of which extolled "the beauty of love" and "the wonders of nature." In the fourth session I confronted her with a more realistic view of men and challenged her to accept them as they were, whether she loved them or not. I explained how her own naiveté had set her up for rejection. She terminated treatment at that point, preferring to see herself as a helpless victim of unknown ugliness.

The more I have worked with hysterical people, the more respect I have for their resistance to change in their basic character style. Helping romantics become more realistic is a slow process indeed. I have had more success forming long-term alliances, in which people call on me periodically to help them again make sense out of their lives. As therapy progresses, they ask about things in their future rather than their past. In helping them use better judgment in making commitments for their future, I have begun to see maturing growth in their character styles.

Another way to help these people is to enlighten their lovers. Tell them how blindly they are being trusted, and what a big disappointment will come for both if they can't be more realistic with each other.

The Seductive Sham. When hysterical characters learn how much attention they can get by acting sexually seductive, look out! Somebody's going to get hurt! On the inside, these people are insecure little children who haven't been given enough attention and genuine love. On the outside, they look charming and attractive. They seem to seduce people into brief casual affairs. The lonelier and more insecure they feel inside, the more obvious their sexy come-ons become. These moves are more likely to attract the very people who use others for their own pleasure. This leaves the unwitting seducers lonelier and more insecure than ever.

Seductive shams are no different from other people on the inside. They enjoy physical affection, and they need to know that they are loved. Their problem is their hysterical style of being aware of only half of these needs at any one time. They yearn for a supportive, secure relationship, only to learn later that they were acting as if they wanted a briefer, more casual affair.

For example, I know a divorced woman who is flirtatious and sexy. Whenever she is at a party, she acts as if she hasn't seen a man in three months. Her eyes dance, her body purrs, and her dramatic chatter is chock full of sexual innuendoes. Underneath that foxy veneer is an extremely chaste young woman. She is just as shocked by a man's pass at her as he is shocked by her rejection of him. She reacts as if to say, "How dare you think such a thing?" Meanwhile he is thinking, "How dare you say no after teasing me like that!" She longs to be recognized for her intelligence, her beauty, her virtues—anything but her steady stream of come-ons. As with a true hysteric, all her perceptions are colored by the one dominant need of the moment. She is completely unaware of how strongly she is expressing her other need for sexual affection.

The exact opposite pattern can also be seen with seductive shams. I know several people whose viewpoints become completely colored with sexual desire. During the romantic chase they have no sense whatever of any nonsexual needs in themselves or their lovers. After lovemaking, they are disappointed to find lots of leftover emotional needs. They advertise themselves as love machines, but they never seem to pull off the total experience. These people use sex to wipe out all their inner tension, much as alcoholics use a cocktail. These seducers ignore their insecurity, but they are just as phony as the naive teases who ignore their sexuality.

To keep from being seduced by such people, you will find it helpful to remember they have one-track minds. They can't be aware simultaneously of both their needs for sexual attention and their needs for loving respect. You have to be very careful not to make the same mistake yourself. The trap is that in sharing your physical affection with each other you will lose sight of your love and respect for each other. Sometimes hysterics see this coming first and pull out, having been through this many times before. You can help them greatly by seeing through it before you have allowed your sexual fantasies to develop too far. You can offer them a caring relationship that sweats out the frustration of sticking to the critical limits on time and touching. It is in this crucible that genuine self-esteem can be discovered.

Within these limits, you can teach them that you love and respect them for who they are down inside, quite apart from their seductive facade. Encourage them to earn their own self-respect by honesty and hard work. Teach them to channel their vast energies into just a few commitments, so they can discover the satisfaction that comes only from being successful in reaching their goals. Allow them to begin being honest with you, and to drop their seductive games of flattery and helplessness. Having discovered that you love and respect them for who they are, they can learn to absorb your positive esteem into their self-concept. By *acting* on that faith in themselves (working hard, being honest, sweating out the loneliness and frustrations), they will no longer have to seduce others for attention, affection, and approval. They will have learned to earn the respect of others, and to *inspire* the love of others. With love and respect, we discover the meaning of these words by St. Francis of Assisi: "For it is in giving that we receive, and it is in dying that we are born to eternal life."

New Ways of Relating to These People

PARANOID STYLES

1. Approach them in a supportive, easygoing, self-reliant way.
2. In a gentle, nonthreatening, and open-minded manner raise doubts and questions about their negative, suspicious view of things.
3. Ask them whether acting on their suspicions might turn these suspicions into self-fulfilling prophecies.
4. Invite them to join you in lighthearted, playful activities.
5. Don't expect them to be very emotional.
6. As a Christian, show them how you forgive people, and how you accept all feelings as human.

OBSESSIVE STYLES

1. Approach them in a lighthearted, spontaneous, humorous, and accepting way.
2. When they get lost in feelings of guilt over the past, let them confess their sins to you. Express your forgiving acceptance, encourage them to forgive themselves, and where appropriate, help them to plan constructive restitution.
3. When they get lost in trivial details, tease them about the

triviality, and restore the focus of attention to more emotionally meaningful questions.

4. When they are weighted down by a sense of duty for the
   future, expose the projection by asking, "Who says you
   have to?"

5. Show them more important and constructive use of their
   time and energy (e.g., their religious faith, their health, the
   welfare of their loved ones, etc.). Worry is such a waste.

HYSTERICAL STYLES

1. Approach them using good judgment, self-control, and
   common sense. Don't let your feelings mislead you.

2. Show them that their emotions are fleeting and shallow,
   and yet intense enough to color thoroughly their view of
   the situation at hand.

3. Don't let them drain you of your three A's—attention,
   affection, and approval, especially when they are acting
   hysterically.

4. Encourage them to decide things not so much on impressions as on reflective judgment.

5. Encourage them to *act* less impulsively, dramatically, and
   demandingly, regardless of how they think or feel.

6. Show them how fleeting is the self-respect that comes
   from producing an attractive veneer. Teach them to *earn*
   self-respect through channeling their vast energies into a
   few solid commitments.

7. Offer a caring relationship that sweats out your resistance
   to the needed limits of time and touching. This allows
   them to discover not *your* strength, but the strength
   within their own souls.

4. Styles of Emotional Response

All people have their own emotional styles, their own way of handling and expressing feelings. With anger, for example, some people may seem to be irritated about something nearly all the time. Their faces may have settled into a perpetual scowl. Others may be inclined to hide their resentments, so that no one ever has the slightest idea that they are angry. These people can be every bit as frustrating to live with as persons in the first group. A third group may occasionally hit both extremes, hiding their anger until the last possible minute, and then surprising everyone by exploding into a fit of rage. These three examples of hot, cold, and unpredictable can be seen with other emotions, such as joy, sadness, and romantic love. The sections of this chapter illustrate examples of these three emotional styles.

AGGRESSIVE STYLES

"I'll give that *#?! just what he deserves!"

There are many ways to pay back a hurt. The Bible mentions several methods that have been acceptable to religions

63

past and present. These do not typically settle into a character style, much less become a disorder. "An eye for an eye" refers to hitting back, repaying an injury immediately, equally, and in kind. "Turning the other cheek," or serving your enemy something nice to eat or drink, can be used to pay back the enemy's hurt by "heaping burning coals (of guilt) upon his head." Still another way is to ask God to settle the score. You can appeal to either his justice (Ps. 28 and 37) or his wrath (Mt. 23) to repay the wrong, or to his mercy and grace to instill love into both you and your enemy. This latter approach of forgiveness is the ideal, both spiritually and psychologically.

The most constructive expression of anger is to put the hurt into words: "It really hurts (bothers, offends, irritates) me when you . . ." Perhaps expressing hurt so directly is difficult for the person with whom you are trying to live. Since expressing feelings often comes so hard for men, let's say this person is a man. Think of him as a pressure cooker about to explode. He could relieve some pressure by exercise and competitive sports or games. But putting his hurt into words would allow you to get a whiff of the steam and guess "what's cooking." You can think of his need to get along with you as the food in the pressure cooker. Then your spirit of acceptance and forgiveness is like the water. The right amount of water in a pressure cooker produces steam, which softens the food and makes it delicious. And so does unconditional love soften and enrich the heart.

The danger is that without enough acceptance and concern, his love for you will begin to dry up, and he will become "burned out" inside. A pressure cooker will explode if the thick, gummy smoke of burning food clogs the pressure valve.

Life supplies the heat—you can turn it up or down a little, but you surely can't turn it off while you live on this earth. What you can do is add the loving concern that enables the heat to soften the aggressive person's heart instead of drying it up.

None of the styles of expressing anger just described are destructive, and they help by quickly identifying hurt and releasing tension. I will mention briefly five other aggressive styles that are not so constructive. They constitute disorders because they tend to escalate the warfare, and because they tend to give such sweet revenge that they become strongly addictive. Thus they tend to set up a vicious cycle, and leave the person further and further alienated.

The Walking Time Bomb. A nice, polite, and soft-spoken man came to me because he was baffled by his inability to control recent fits of jealous rage. By his demeanor, values, and life-style he seemed one of the gentlest men I had ever met. But whenever he felt backed into a corner, he suddenly became violently angry, breaking things and cursing people at the top of his lungs. These outbursts had been known to occur when he was in a crowd, alone with his lover, or enjoying a quiet evening with a few friends. What was striking about this man was his inability to control the explosions, and the guilt and remorse he felt almost immediately afterward.

These human time bombs are among the most common types of character disorder I see in therapy. I've seen many men and women with this explosive style, and quite a few children especially around the age of seven or eight. The first step in working with these people is to rule out a seizure disorder due to a physical dysfunction of the brain. A neurologist, psychiatrist, family physician, or mental health center is likely to screen for this type of seizure by taking a careful history and getting an EEG (brain-wave reading). If these signs point to some form of epilepsy, anticonvulsant medication can often bring dramatic relief of symptoms.

One other physical cause of such outbursts can be alcohol or drug abuse. Many explosive people turn to these substances in order to relieve their pressure and prevent explosions, only to find that the cure becomes a curse and secretly undermines their self-control. These people must be helped over their addictions *first*, ideally through a group such as Alcoholics Anonymous.

You can help human time bombs learn to prevent explosions. These people are usually down on themselves, even though they may seem quite the opposite. The first step is to support who they are apart from the explosions. Hold fast to the faith that they can learn to change, and very much want to change, deep down inside. Then try to identify the type of pressure they allow to build within them. Is it the fear of failure or of hurting others? Is it the desire to please others and make them proud? Is it the fear of being left alone? Is it the desire to earn and deserve all the love that they get? Once you have identified "what's cooking," you can help them see how much of the pressure is self-inflicted.

After they see how much of the pressure is self-generated, there are three ways they can deal with it. First, they can avoid the situations that cause pressure, at least for a while. They can start "taking the heat off" themselves until they can cope with their anger. Second, they can use their pressure valve, to "blow off steam" with some of the constructive outlets mentioned at the first of this chapter. Finally, they can associate with the accepting, caring, and forgiving people in their church, family, or circle of friends. Such relationships can soften them and enable more pressure to be absorbed without drying up and losing touch with others.

How should you yourself respond to the person's explosions? Limits must be set on how much damage can be done to relationships with you. It is essential for the relationship to continue for the sake of the person you seek to help, so you have to know what your limits are, and make sure they are protected. If you are a battered or frightened wife, you may have to get a legal separation, a restraining order, a peace bond, or an unlisted phone number in order to prevent your husband from wrecking your life and killing your desire to help him.

The Avenger of Social Injustice. A man once came to me complaining that he could not hold his temper with his wife. When his anger started to build, he would get so angry that he couldn't help slapping her around and calling her awful names. He hated himself for being unable to control himself. But unlike the human time bomb, this man sported an air of self-righteousness. He always believed his victim had it coming.

When asked what triggered these violent outbursts, he said it was always a discussion of some moral issue such as child abuse or abortion. He felt so keenly the hurt of a rejected child that he was personally going to even the score. He could not forgive his wife's having once had an abortion before marriage, or her love affair with a child-abusing man. Nor could he forgive her parents, who had secretly condoned abortions for her sisters. The hardest pill of all to swallow was when some of these sinners turned around, cleaned up their act, and won great acceptance in the church and community for their professed moral purity. He told me that he felt bitter toward God for letting the hypocrisy go unexposed, the immorality go unpunished. So he took the law of God into his own hands and decided to inflict continual punishment on his wife and her family. When it became apparent that he was losing his wife and daughter, he tried to stop but found that he couldn't. Eventually his wife divorced him and he lost custody of his daughter. He couldn't even find a church home because he kept looking down on everybody in the church for their secret faults. He himself felt morally pure, and played the martyr much like the elder brother in Jesus' story of the prodigal son.

The only way I know to work with people like this is to wait until their bubble bursts. You can help to prick it by pointing out their own lack of self-control, the hurt they have inflicted on others, and especially how they are playing God. But chances are they won't let you get that close unless you can show some love and respect for the person underneath the Lone Ranger mask. Offer comfort and understanding for the many hurts they have sustained during their crusade. Recognize the noble aspect of their goal to repay and reform the other self-righteous offenders of the world.

Change for this man came when he realized that he couldn't control his temper and avoid losing his wife and daughter. The final straw was his seeing that he was failing miserably at playing God—the more he tried to right the wrongs, the more he suffered and the less his wife and her family suffered. His victims would not put up with him and his wife filed for divorce. This put him at rock bottom, and from there he joined AA to stop his drinking, became involved in a forgiving church community, and began to take God up on the offer: "Vengeance is mine—I will repay."

The Malicious Gossip. A variation of the crusading martyr we just described is the person who expresses anger by spreading bad news, true and untrue. The funny thing about these people is that I seldom see one in my office—it's always their victims, the walking wounded of the verbal warfare carried on behind their backs. I know several of these malicious gossips in church and social groups.

The key to dealing with these people is to realize you can't beat them at their own game. They have usually formed little squadrons of fellow rumormongers who stick together for protection. They have begun more and more to look down on those outside the group. You can begin to cut into their character style by cutting off the flow of information. Get friends and family to stop feeding them bad news, and especially to stop listening to it.

If more drastic measures are required, the best bet is to work on the group. If they are in the church, talk about it openly, tell the group how they are sinning according to the Bible. Perhaps you can help them to see how they are doing much more harm than good with their gossip.

On a one-to-one basis, it is often difficult to tell if a person sharing with you a juicy piece of news is doing so in a spirit of genuine concern or one of malicious gossip. One good way to identify a gossiping spirit is to ask questions like these: "Why are you telling me this news about Mildred?"; "How will it help her for you to tell me?" (watch for a flattering answer here); "Wouldn't she rather be the one to tell me?"; and "What can we do to help Mildred?"

The Passive Aggressor. I was once one of the best around at this game. I call the game "P.A." for passive aggression. I am not recommending the game, but ask yourself if you are a passive aggressor. When someone makes you angry, you hold in all your anger and just do nothing. It's like a sit-down strike. By being passive and doing nothing, you make the other person furious. You keep playing the game until the person gives up.

I learned to play this game from my father. His greatest accomplishment came one afternoon some thirty years ago at the bridge table with my mother. He finally made her so angry that she (God love her!) dumped a lemon meringue pie right on top of his head. Dad didn't say a word, and without removing one bit of pie from his head or clothes, he quietly and politely insisted that everyone go on with the bridge game. He never said another word to my mother until they got home, and then he said, "Now don't you think you made a bit of a fool out of yourself?" The amazing thing is that until the last few years, my mother would tell this story as if it had all been her fault. Now they've both changed their style, thank goodness.

The way I used to be a passive aggressor was with my wife, Molly. When I would hurt her in some way, she would naturally tell me about it and expect me to stop it. But the mere suggestion of anger or blame in her voice would make me furious and very defensive. Through the first two years of our marriage, I learned to play P.A. like a champ. Nothing—but nothing—could make me raise my voice. Whenever Molly would raise her voice to challenge me, I would come back with a sweet little comment like "Oh, I'm sorry, dear. I didn't realize you were so sensitive about that." This would usually frustrate her even more, because I obviously felt no remorse. I was asking her to be less sensitive. She would then get angrier and raise her voice more. I would start to smell victory and make some comment like: "Honey, you're getting upset now. I didn't mean to hurt you." A later move might be: "Now you're making an absolute fool of yourself. Why don't you calm down and discuss this like an adult?" Finally I wouldn't have to say a thing—I could just sit back and enjoy watching her climb the walls or pull her hair out.

It is not easy to help passive aggressors to change their style. You are asking them to give up a game they never lose, one they seldom if ever realize they are playing. Trying to convince them that they were angry in a given situation is useless. You are more likely to get results by suggesting that they don't know *how* to get angry, or won't let themselves. The characters who have come to think of anger as a sin need to read Mk. 3:5; Matthew 23; and Eph. 4:26. Somehow they must come to see how to express their anger in a mature, verbal way ("That hurts me!"; "I can't stand it when you . . ."; etc.). It helps if they can realize that until they can learn to express themselves in this way, they cannot fully succeed in their marriage or career.

During graduate school, I had to go into psychotherapy for a few months. All my supervisors got together to tell me what I needed. "Schmidt, you'll never be a good therapist until you can recognize and respond to anger. You are completely blind to the anger your clients are expressing toward you in their behavior and remarks. You can't even see the classical signs of anger in your client's Rorschach inkblot responses. Your own Rorschach is full of aggressive indicators, and yet you say it must all be under the surface. What happens when you and your wife argue?" In therapy I learned that there was no absolute strength or weakness with emotions—someone strong enough to hold them in or deny them is really too weak to risk experiencing and expressing them.

So, if your husband is a passive aggressor and you want to change his style, you have to beat him at his own game. Make him look weak instead of strong, childish and foolish instead of mature and wise. Or, give him a taste of his own medicine and stage a sit-down strike of your own. But be careful to support him when his anger finally comes out—it's likely to be in a rather immature, awkward way. He may be ugly or mean at first, until he learns how to control himself. Be sure to give him his right to be angry. Comfort his hurt, even while you are setting limits on how violent he can be in the way he expresses himself.

A good example of supportive limits is what occurred in our marriage midway through my four months of therapy. I finally opened up my storehouse of anger one night and pushed my wife out of bed. She quickly retreated to the kitchen. Sensing my newfound power to frighten her into listening, I decided to follow her into the kitchen and hold her by the shoulders until she agreed with me. But when I rounded the corner into the kitchen, I was stopped dead in my tracks by the look in her eyes. Every nerve and muscle in her body was urging me to stop. She somehow knew that my pushing her around could only happen *once* in our home. I had just used up that option completely. I am grateful for the courage and wisdom she showed in that moment. I calmly backed up and we had a good two-hour discussion sitting twelve feet apart on the living room floor. She was supportive of my anger and my hurt, but not of my pushing her around. Her response has made it easier for me to express my hurts, but it will be many moons before I push that person out of bed again!

Apathetic Styles

"I'm too tired— and what difference would it make anyway?"

Being emotional is being spontaneous. It is letting life affect you as it affects a child—without trying to control life too much by analyzing it. To experience your emotions helps you greatly to understand life, and to be able to flow with a feeling deeply enriches your enjoyment of life. So people whose feelings are blunted and blocked off are often regarded as pitiful and dull by others.

Experiencing a feeling is kind of like hearing a good joke —one often leads quickly and unpredictably to another. Many people think of their emotions as a Pandora's box— open up your feelings and you never know what kind of monster will come out. It is true that emotions have an ebb and flow that defies control and analysis. It is hard to shut off one feeling without soon finding your other feelings becoming a bit flat and empty.

Many spiritual leaders and social scientists alike are saying that apathy is America's greatest social problem. "I just don't care anymore," America is saying. "I could *give* a damn."

There are lots of different ways to achieve and maintain apathy, and I'll give examples of some of the better-known styles.

The Loner. Of all styles of apathy, the hardest to change is the loner. The loner has built a safe shell around a deep mistrust of the one source of rescue from his or her prison— people. The loner sees all people as wanting to use others for their own gain. These attitudes toward people are usually learned in the first few years of life, and are reinforced by parents who train their children in strategic retreat from all of life's hurts and fears. Typically the parents teach children that only they really understand, love, or tolerate them. When the parents then turn around and use, abuse, or betray them, the result is a deep mistrust of all people. These kids become hardhearted people who seem to be in business for themselves.

Loners generally have not experienced a satisfactory, close personal relationship, and have stopped looking for one. The best way to reach these people is to establish yourself as a reliable provider of something the loner needs. In learning to trust you to provide food or entertainment or whatever, slowly you will be trusted for other things. But you must be careful to let the loner set the pace, and this generally takes years.

The Pseudo-Intellectual. Colleges seem to attract people who forever analyze all their emotions and turn them into thoughts that can be controlled. This process can lead to an addictive, sterile self-absorption. One of my clients called this "analysis paralysis," and another referred to it as "navel gazing." These people profess to love their emotions, but they don't love to experience them. They just love to think about them, and in the process they think all the spontaneity and life out of them. Many people with this emotional style turn out to be psychologists who write books.

The guru who has enlightened many such souls on campus is Fritz Perls, and his book *In and Out of the Garbage Pail* (1971) is recommended reading for those intellectuals who want to change. Reading books, by the way, is the primary way these people prepare to change. Actual change usually comes at a time of crisis. Most urban churches are aware of groups designed for "human growth potential" or "self-awareness." Weekend church retreats are ideal for bringing these people out. In any case, the key is to follow up the intellectual's initial response of opening up, by continuing the experience of emotional dialogue into the weeks and months that follow.

The Social Parasite. These are the people which upper-middle-class fathers refer to as a "drain on society." Later in the evening they may be called bums, or lazy so-and-sos. The only thing they work hard at is avoiding work. You know the answer they· want to hear when they greet you with "You workin' hard, or hardly workin'?" You may find them on food stamps or welfare rolls. But they can also have a high-status, low-profile job in a big organization. Or they can be young people wanting to live off their parents' money for as long as possible. Most of these rich bums have had a good model to follow in a father who likes to cheat in his business, or a mother who makes it her business to hire out all her domestic responsibilities to servants, restaurants, or cleaning services.

All these people are social parasites because they get by on the efforts of others whenever possible.

To change their lazy character styles, there is no use trying to shame them. They are proud of their accomplishments, and they believe you should be ashamed of yourself for working so hard when you could enjoy life as they do. A more productive approach is to cut their money off. Derail the gravy train if you can. Expect some work and sense of responsibility before you give them any of your support. If this means putting junior on an allowance with household chores, the sooner the better. A fixed budget and car privileges will spur him to find a job. A spendthrift spouse may need to experience rationing.

"Poor Me." Have you ever known anyone who has made a life-style out of self-pity? Feeling sorry for oneself focuses on limited opportunities and tough breaks. These people explain their miserable fates as bad luck, and see themselves as victims of circumstance. They say they are looking for life to give them that one lucky break they need to get started, but their lives have demonstrated that they wouldn't know a good opportunity if they saw one. They are really looking for a sure bet, a handout on a silver platter. This character style regularly shows up at the church door in traveling from town to town looking for a handout. Whereas the social parasite plays on the hard work of others, the "poor me" plays on their sympathies. Eric Berne has written about the game of "Wooden Leg" that people play—"How can you expect me to do that with this wooden leg?" They wear their handicaps and hardships like merit badges. One danger of this life-style is that these people begin to believe their own hard-luck

stories, and they can become bitter and pessimistic as time goes on.

Such people are most difficult to help, because they have come to doubt their own abilities without realizing it. Hard luck is easier to accept than laziness and failure, and so they are reluctant to assume any responsibility for their misery. But as with the social parasites, the most reliable road to recovery is for others to stop bailing them out. You can throw them a rope, but if they don't pull themselves out of the swamp, they will slide right back in as soon as you let go of your end of the rope.

Temperamental Styles

"These highs and lows just carry me away."

Just as the emotional pendulum swings back and forth between gentle love and violent hatred, so does it swing between joy and sadness. Kahlil Gibran has said, "Your joy is your sorrow unmasked" *(The Prophet).* He suggests that our experience of sorrow reflects our potential for experiencing joy, and vice versa. The character style becomes disordered when the person seeks to dwell in perpetual joy or perpetual sorrow, actively excluding the other emotion. Or, a person may adopt an unstable style that seems always to bounce from one extreme to the other. All these styles are disordered, in that these people seldom form satisfying relationships with themselves or other people.

Fits of Melancholy. I well remember a woman who came into my office one morning and poured out such a tale of woe

I could hardly keep back the tears. Three different husbands had divorced her, and she said, "I have no idea why—I guess because I'm so ugly." Both her parents had died within a few months of each other, and she described her siblings as always looking down on her and refusing to give her any help. She described life for herself and her children as crawling out of one pit only to fall into another.

When she left my office, I felt so sorry for her that I called several people to try to pull together some help for her. From them I found out that trying to help her was like pouring oneself down a drain. Her sad story was the story of her life, her character style. To pick herself up, she would apparently do no more than alternate between plans A, B, C, and SOS —alcohol, binge eating, cheap sex, and trying to turn on the savior fantasy of some sucker like me.

The most obvious things about these pitiful people are their severely depressed moods and lack of self-esteem. They and others fall into a trap when they try to pump up the mood, but this is like trying to blow up a balloon that has a slow leak. Like the balloon, there's something wrong with the character style—it won't hold joy. The character would do much better to work on habits of thinking and behavior. The woman I saw needed to chuck plans A, B, C, and SOS, and begin doing things that build up her self-esteem (working hard, devoting herself to her children, improving her appearance, and committing herself to the life of a church). She needed to stop thinking of herself as a victim awaiting her next cruel twist of fate. She needed to think instead about the good things that could happen in the future if she would avoid the old behaviors that had done her in before.

If you are trying to be a companion to such people, I

suggest that you change your style of relating to them. Dedicate yourself to *enjoying them* when you are together. If this means teasing them or changing the subject when they begin to play the Lonely Hearts Club violin, then do it. Don't let yourself get sucked into the downer's hole. Allow your own optimism and enthusiasm to draw people into your enjoyment of life. If they refuse, say good-by and try again next time.

Carried Away with Themselves (the Mood Swingers). What we call a "manic episode" is marked by boundless energy, a grossly inflated self-esteem, a bubbly mood, and an optimism for the future that is blown out of all proportion. Constantly talking, moving, and smiling, these people seem to be high on something. They are very charming at first impression, but soon they begin to strain our credibility, drain our patience, and empty our pocketbooks. These episodes can be caused by drugs, brain infections, or manic-depressive psychosis, and examination by a physician should be made to rule out these conditions.

But like the melancholic character we just looked at, some people use fits of elation to gloss over and avoid dealing with the realities of their lives. Getting carried away takes them away from the conflicts inside them, and from the people around them who are trying to get close to them.

I have worked with a couple of people near the age of twenty who both admitted that their main purpose in life was being as emotionally high as possible at all times. One was a young man who was spending his days driving at high speeds back and forth from one city to another. The other was a young woman who bounced back and forth between brief relationships that were intensely charged with sex and emotion. Both loved the feeling of speeding through life, but both agreed that they were going in circles. As you might have guessed, both were into drugs. But in both cases their drug use was episodic—they would often quit for a period of time, only to find the same craving to "get off on something—sex, drugs, love, anything." They could stay away from drugs, but they would always get off on something else. What they couldn't do was handle tension. Neither could tolerate the strain of knowing that his or her behavior was hurting someone else.

When they were high (which was most of the time), both were attractive people. They seemed intelligent, kind, ambitious, and sexually alive. Their self-esteem seemed to be up in the clouds somewhere. But both had increasingly frequent episodes of bottoming out—their egos would burst and they would find themselves in the pits, hating themselves bitterly.

How in the world can you sustain a relationship with such flighty, up-and-down people? First you must ensure that you don't let them take advantage of you—don't depend on them for anything. You must remember they are seldom as great or as worthless as they think they are at the time. Their real selves are in the middle between the highs and lows. You stand in the middle and call out to them to come down or up to meet you in reality. In relating to you, they gradually get back in touch with their own centers of self-worth. With you they can struggle with the dualities of being great but insignificant, a passionate thinker but a dispassionate doer, capable of reaching the heights but unable to shake loose from the pits. Help these people see themselves not only as immortal souls but also as members of the human family, seeking to enjoy fellowship within the limits of time and space.

If you stay in touch with both their dreams and their limits at all times, you are in touch with the frustration they are running from. When they are up, you can keep them in touch with the limits of time, money, and the energy of their bodies. When they are down, remind them of their dreams. Tell them how their lack of time, money, energy, and self-esteem are temporary overdrafts, not basic inadequacies. In their better moments, you can help them bring their dreams into focus by asking how much time and money will be required, where it will come from, etc. It is good for them also to establish an overriding dream, one around which they can build their life. This dream will be the first thing to pull them up from the depths.

I have also found it productive to help them focus on their attitude toward their bodies. They are likely to see the body as a prison for their spirits, or a ball and chain holding them back in their race through life. The mood swingers I have worked with have been liberated by viewing their bodies as instruments they use in pursuing their dream in this life. As with a well-tuned car, the better they take care of it, the more it can do for them. Wearing it out with chemical, sexual, or emotional highs makes it blow a gasket and run out of gas.

Finally, these people tune in to the here and now. They aren't too concerned about yesterday or tomorrow, and they probably never will be. They *can* change what they look for in each moment. Rather than seeking the rush of a high, they can learn to value the solid sense of personal integrity. Flowing together as body, soul, and spirit is a high that builds them up. Here they find true exhilaration without exhaustion. This dream of feeling together becomes more and more a reality each day that they chase it.

New Ways of Relating to These People

AGGRESSIVE STYLES

1. Approach them with calmness, forgiveness, and faith in your own self-worth.
2. Rule out physical causes for outbursts (seizures, drugs, alcohol, etc.).
3. Don't let them take advantage of your fear. Back up your limits by separation and/or legal help.
4. Teach them to use more constructive outlets for anger (and be sure to use these yourself): prayer, forgiveness, killing with kindness, and—ideally—putting hurt feelings into words.
5. Identify the pressure they are feeling. Show them how they are pressuring themselves, and how to let off steam.
6. Reduce your expectations of them enough that you aren't too hurt to forgive them. Raise your expectations enough that you believe they can change.
7. With gossips, don't tell or listen to rumors or suspicions. Question their motives for telling you of other people's shortcomings.
8. Give passive aggressors a taste of their own medicine. Your passivity and calmness will lead them to their own motivation.

APATHETIC STYLES

1. Approach them with cheerful, humorous optimism, *without* feeling sorry for them.

2. Relate to what they *do* care about, and don't get too worked up over what they *don't* care about.
3. Get lazy people off your gravy train. Make them *earn* what you do for them. Don't give them too much attention or assistance when they are passive.
4. Don't pretend to be their savior. Tell them that only God can meet all their needs, and that even God works through their answering his call to faith and service.

TEMPERAMENTAL STYLES

1. Approach them by giving attention and expression to your own feelings, but use your mind and soul to keep your heart from getting lost in their highs and lows.
2. With people in the pits, teach them how to build self-esteem through developing habits of positive thinking, unselfish action, wholesome fun, and prayers for help.
3. With people on a prolonged and uncontrollable high, suggest an examination by a physician. Ask questions about their limits of time, money, and energy.
4. With mood swingers, show them that you sense the tension and conflict between their noble dreams and their inconsistent performance.

5. Styles of Behavior

This chapter describes people whose character styles are dominated by their habits. The ways they *act* under stress alienate them from others, and often from themselves as well. Compulsive people tend to drive themselves constantly. They respond to tension by pressuring themselves to perform better. Impulsive people respond to inner conflict by suddenly "acting out" one of their impulses, thus transferring some of their anxiety to others who worry about what they will do next. Their character styles are disordered, because these behaviors only increase the problems they already have in managing their physical tension and personal relationships.

COMPULSIVE STYLES

"But I *have* to do it, and I have to do it right."

Wilhelm Reich, in his book *Character Analysis,* described compulsive people well as "living machines," continually being driven to perform faster and better. The problem is that they feel pressured by a strong sense of duty, either so vague or so urgent that they seem helpless to throw the burden off and say no. Though they feel the pressure as coming from others, they are actually pressing themselves without knowing it.

The behavior of these people strikes others as rigid and tightly controlled. This stiffness often extends to their posture, muscle tone, gestures, and facial expressions. They tend to develop habits that strongly resist change or spontaneous variation. For example, habits of personal hygiene or getting dressed may become fixed into definite routines that they observe religiously.

Their behavior also tends to be intense, and almost hyperactive. They seem to be in constant motion. Many seem to possess boundless energy, at least until they exhaust themselves. They keep themselves always busy doing something— sorting, counting, arranging, rearranging, cleaning, and re-cleaning. They seem utterly incapable of goofing off.

It's not just how much they do that strikes you. It's also the way they do it. Everything is planned, controlled, and deliberate. They don't stop and get in touch with what they *want* to do, because they are forever distracted by what they *should* do. To experience a wish or desire would undermine their work output. There is no time for silly things like laughing, crying, yawning, or even resting for a few minutes. Like robots, they cannot operate under mixed instructions from the world outside, and there is no room for whims or feelings inside either. Compulsive people will tolerate no interference from within or without. They keep themselves busy in single-minded fashion, lowering their heads and trudging on like a tethered ox or a harnessed mule.

The approach I have used to deal with these people is to tell them that they have an obligation to their families which demands that they spend time playing and relaxing, even if they have to suffer through it at first. I had to challenge one perfectionist fellow by betting him that he could not endure, much less enjoy, playing checkers with me. Fortunately, he won the bet, and then discovered that he could enjoy bowling with his wife.

For the compulsive person who has already begun to wonder whether he or she *should* change, and especially for people who have begun to realize they *want* to unwind a bit, I strongly recommend Wayne Oates's recent book, *Workaholics: Make Laziness Work for You* (1978). I have also found it fruitful to discuss the meaning of Jesus' words in Luke 10, where he calls the relaxed enjoyment of Mary "more important" than the compulsive hard work of her sister Martha.

The Hard Driver. The most common example of the compulsive style is found in the people who drive themselves continually to keep up with the musts and the shoulds in their heads. Despite the basic similarities of their drive-shaft backbones, it is surprising how much variety they exhibit in the way they live their lives.

On the one hand, a woman complained of breakdowns in her relationships with her husband and her children. Yet they told me how she had some serious health problems that she had never told me about. Although her husband brought in a good income, she not only held a full-time job, she also worked four nights a week at another job. While around the house, she continually tried to wash or straighten out something, so that there simply wasn't time to enjoy her family. Oh yes! She also gave some six hours a week to the church, which her family begrudged considerably, and did volunteer work another four hours each week at a hospital. As is so often seen with compulsive people, she stubbornly defended each activity as something she simply had to do. The amazing thing was her inability to understand why her family didn't love and appreciate her for all the wonderful things she was *doing*. They just wanted her to enjoy *being* at home with them. As is often the case, she had learned this style during a Cinderella type of childhood. She was the oldest child of many, expected to stay constantly busy cleaning and baby-sitting, while her peers and siblings were having normal child-hood play experiences. Unfortunately she dropped out of treatment, feeling guilty about the time and money she was spending on herself.

Another example of a hard driver is a young man who came to me as a college sophomore, complaining of tension head-aches and backaches. He expected himself to make great grades, and to have made a final choice on a vocation as a freshman. Whenever he had fun, he would feel guilty after-ward. When asked about the pressure, he said he wished his parents and professors would push him more, so that he would study more and commit himself to a vocation. He has found help in disciplining himself to go through some relaxation exercises for thirty minutes each day. He has also benefited greatly from observing the fourth commandment to keep the Sabbath day free from the demands of work.

Still another hard driver I have known looks remarkably different on the outside. She was once as busy as anybody, but she has now developed the empty nest syndrome. She also fights the pressure in her small, affluent, Southern town, which tells her that a woman's place is in the home. No one expects her to do anything useful anymore, and so she is bored stiff staying at home. Most women in this town enjoy their leisure time, but she is a hard driver at heart. She hates herself for doing nothing, and her body is constantly pulling at itself to get her going. As a result, she suffers from several physical problems her doctors say are "from nerves." So even when she's sitting still she drives herself inside, to guilt over the past, resentment of the present, and worry about the future. My advice to her has been to straighten out her steering wheel, so that she is going in some constructive direction instead of spinning her mental wheels and going in circles. The more she works to meet the needs of her family, friends, and church, the better she feels about herself. And the better she feels about herself, the more she is able to relax and enjoy life in her spare time.

The White Tornado. You have probably seen on TV commercials the finicky mother-in-law, the woman who checks for dust with white gloves, or the woman grinning from ear to ear as she wipes the Lysol off her sparkling toilet bowl. Cleaning is a favorite pastime for compulsives, but not all people who keep spotless houses have a character disorder. It's only those who habitually use their cleaning and busywork to avoid dealing with worries or people.

Your efforts to make them stop cleaning will probably be "fruitile" (fruitless and futile). You'll probably have better luck trying to talk with them while they clean, or teasing them about how unnecessary and wasteful it all is. Their pride tells them, If cleanliness is so important to me, it should be to everybody. As long as "cleanliness is next to godliness," they are going to get what they pay for—a sterile home where nobody else feels comfortable.

The Sneakin' Deacon. It is surprising how often I have counseled religious, upstanding people, who come to me deeply embarrassed because they have been caught in some isolated immoral act that is totally out of character for them. One woman regarded as a model Christian was caught repeatedly shoplifting things she could have paid for easily. I have worked with several seminary students who were caught exposing themselves. These acts on the surface seem impulsive, but the life-style of these people is not at all impulsive. They are persons driven by duty and guilt, who usually act in a disciplined, deliberate way. Though these acts are not the deliberate and socially acceptable behaviors compulsives usually show, they are nonetheless driven to do them, and the behaviors serve to reduce the tension built up by a compulsive life-style.

To tell the deacon to stop his sneakin' is to make matters worse—he already tells himself to stop it a hundred times a day. These people are terribly ashamed of themselves, but they find the more they pressure themselves not to do something, the more they do it. To break out of the cycle they must start changing their compulsive life-styles. Once they see the need for this, they usually make rapid progress.

When the problems have been sexual, there has usually been great pressure to perform in their sexual lives. One young man would announce to his wife in the morning that they would make it that night when the kids went to bed. All day he would feel the pressure, wondering if he was going to perform adequately. To make sure his equipment would not malfunction in an emergency, he rehearsed ways to arouse himself quickly through various wild fantasies such as flashing total strangers. It is amazing how surprised people are when they suddenly act out fantasies that have excited them many times before.

Once the actual performance started at home with his wife, every move was calculated and rehearsed. He felt totally responsible for arousing her, presenting a durable erection, and going through whatever routines seemed necessary to bring her to climax. What was absolutely missing from their love life was spontaneity and teasing.

Like the other Christian flashers, this young man found great relief when his wife came in with him to help take the pressure off sexually. Casual teasing outside the bedroom has helped a lot—a pat while passing in the hall, a playful smile or innuendo at the dinner table, etc. They have also found it helpful to reduce the pressures to perform in nonsexual areas of their lives by learning to relax and say no to excessive demands on their time.

IMPULSIVE STYLES

"All of a sudden something came over me and I just *did* it."

Persons with impulsive character disorders tend to act suddenly on their whims and desires without using much judgment or forethought. Their behavior is generally loose—free from anxiety, frustration, and inhibition. They act as if they are always a little bit tipsy. I remember how all the entertainers in Honolulu urged us to "hang loose." This is a way of life for impulsive people. They have a very low tolerance for frustration, and they seldom show stable commitments to people, organizations, goals, or values. They are uninhibited nearly all the time, and they feel O.K. about it.

Their thinking tends to be like their behavior—loose, quick, passive, unintentional, and impressionistic. In addition, their thinking is usually quite concrete, dealing almost exclusively with the impressions of the eyes and ears. They seldom think about the abstract questions of what these impressions mean. There is an absence of planning before they act, and of reflecting afterward in order to learn from the experience. Lacking a sense of deliberate intention prior to their actions, they see the responsibility and control for their behavior as outside themselves. If you present an impulsive person with an opportunity for immediate pleasure, it will be seized as soon as it is seen. There is no intermediate step of thinking, "I sure would like to have one of those doughnuts . . . now what will I do?" The thinking would be more like, "There's something fun, so I'll do it."

Living with these people is a real challenge. It's like taking a two-year-old boy into a china shop. You walk in and right on his eye level he spots some delicate, expensive, little Cybis figurines. The only way to deal with this is either not to let him walk around in the shop, or else to follow him so closely that as soon as he sees something, you can step in and prevent his acting on impulse. Much like the two-year-old, impulsive people don't feel responsible for controlling their behavior. It's apparently impossible for them to recall a choice point prior to their actions. It's unlikely that they can change their

basic character style to the point where they routinely stop
and reason before they act.

There are basically two ways to deal with their stimulus-
response style of behavior. One is to change the stimulus, and
thereby limit the kinds of temptations they must face. If an
impulsive man drinks too much at cocktail parties, he could
decide not to go, or to avoid the bar and let his wife get drinks
for him. A man who dislikes the way he is drawn into the gay
world could avoid driving downtown alone. A man who finds
himself impulsively getting into fistfights can avoid going into
bars without someone who understands his problem and is big
enough to restrain him.

The other way to deal with this behavior is to change the
response to the stimulus. Some impulsive persons are both-
ered by one particular behavior (like drinking) brought on by
a known type of stimulus (like the sight of a bottle). If they
want to change their behavior, they can get help from one of
the many university psychology clinics that have programs of
behavior modification. For example, one program for homosexuals who want to change their behavior shows them various arousing scenes with a slide projector. When the scene is
homosexually oriented, the subject agrees to receive immediately a mild electric shock, or something else unpleasant. If
the scene shows someone of the opposite sex, there is no
punishment, and the subject's fantasies and reactions are his
own reward. Similar programs for impulsive alcoholics use a
simulated bar to modify drinking behavior, or a pill that
causes vomiting if alcohol is swallowed. The results of these
programs are good for those who are serious enough in wanting to change their behavior to follow the exercises of the
program.

Impulsive persons often do not want to change their behavior, much less work at it hard enough to cooperate by doing therapeutic homework exercises. For these people, you may have to be the one providing immediate punishment for the behavior you want to change. Laugh at the flasher. Smack the man who pinches your derriere at a party. A person who hits you in a fit of rage should be left alone, or forced to leave you alone. Once is the first and last time. Victims of spouse abuse usually have to go somewhere else (a spouse abuse center, for example). Eventually they may have to file charges and ask for a peace bond before the abusers change their ways.

The Short Fuse. Spouse abusers and suddenly violent people come in several varieties. I have already described the Walking Time Bomb and the Avenger of Social Injustice. The explosive violence of the Short Fuse looks the same on the outside, but underneath there is neither the avenger's consciously premeditated choice nor the sense of guilt and shame the time bomb feels. Although time bombs also act impulsively, this is not a style of life for them. They at least know what deliberate, intentional behavior is, and they know the experience of not letting themselves do something they want to do at the time. When they compare these acts of judgment and restraint with their temper outbursts, they feel guilty. But unlike time bombs, short fuses are impulsive with all of their whimsical desires, not just the angry ones. They can't imagine restraining themselves with such a strong urge, so they feel no guilt.

When two-year-olds hit or break things, most people spank them or confine them in their rooms for a while. These short fuses are acting like two-year-olds, and they need the same

treatment (immediate punishment and restriction of privileges). If this can't be done in the community, I suggest that
you press charges and let the judge decide what will teach
them how unacceptable their behavior is. Usually a fine or a
restraining order will help, but in severe cases a correctional
institution may be needed for a time. An institution can give
both the restrictions needed to protect society, and the ongo-
ing, immediate consequences necessary for learning to change
their impulsive behavior.

The Overcautious Dropout. These people give in to their
passive impulses, not their active ones. The urges to quit their
jobs, stay silent, go to sleep, or stay at home overwhelm them.
Mental health professionals call these people passive personalities. On the surface, they aren't flamboyant and uninhibited like the other impulsive characters I have described
in this section. But they are alike in the sense that they cannot
say no to a strong impulse from within. Therefore, rather than
become so involved in a situation that they can't help acting
out their desires, they prefer to avoid embarrassment and live
on the fringes of life.

They may also have one or two active impulses which they
have trouble resisting, such as eating, drinking, or masturbat-
ing. They will typically describe these behaviors as resulting
from moments of weakness, a breakdown of their willpower.
But there is a difference between these impulsive acts and
those of the short fuse. Overcautious dropouts usually see
themselves as being overwhelmed by pressure from the situation, not from their own desires within. They have tried so
hard to avoid such temptations that they can't imagine how
such awful thoughts could arise from within their souls. They

act like paranoids, and see the immoral monsters as "out there" somewhere in the environment. And so they use their fears as excuses to keep from getting involved. "The lazy man is full of excuses. 'I can't go to work!' he says. 'If I go outside I might meet a lion in the street and be killed!' " (Prov. 22:13, Living Bible).

So how can you encourage these dropouts to discipline themselves and start taking chances again? They are like young children who stand in the corner and watch others play games. You've got to make it less comfortable in the corner, *and* more comfortable getting involved. Just criticizing them for their behavior will only add to their insecurity. Ask them what they are afraid of, and guide them to ask if perhaps they fear their own impulsiveness most of all. If they need help identifying which impulses they fear, they can either talk to a professional about it or get more involved and find out from experience.

Just as body building takes disciplined work as one lifts heavier and heavier weights, character building for passive people takes practice too. If they will let you stay by their side and help them avoid acting impulsively, they can learn to handle more and more emotional involvement. Make a deal with them—if they go to a party, a job interview, a church function, or whatever, agree to stay by their side until they want to leave you. Your coaching and encouraging them not to act on their impulses can give them the wisdom and strength they need to start enjoying life again.

The Pathological Liar. One behavior that lends itself nicely to impulsive acting out is lying. Like other impulsive acts, it serves to reduce inner tension. It takes the heat off the psyche by disarming the conscience in its battle against our natural urges. But unlike other impulsive acts, lying can often keep our urge from being detected or reported. When we do get caught in an act, a lie can sometimes keep us from being convicted of intentional wrongdoing. So to a person who wants to avoid involvement, a lie is a pretty handy thing. As with other impulsive persons, it helps to treat the pathological liar like a child who has not yet learned to control himself. With a five-year-old boy who lies about his mistakes, you can first of all give him permission to make mistakes without punishment. You would reward each confession of a private transgression by loving him and trusting him more to report on himself. This positive approach is almost essential in drawing out honest behavior. A positive, supportive atmosphere makes brief negative consequences much more effective. Support teaches the liar that you are acting in his behalf, that you are *for* him and not against him. Then he can understand why you restrict his privileges when you have reason to suspect that he has not been truthful with you. This is the way the boy who cried wolf learned to stop lying, and I haven't discovered a better way yet.

Rest assured there is much that can be done with impulsive people. Because of his faith in Jesus, it was the impetuous Peter who was chosen to head the church after Jesus' resurrection. Peter had proven his impulsive nature by sudden acts in which he used poor judgment—trying to walk on water, forbidding Jesus to suffer and die, and interrupting the voice of God at the transfiguration. But he saved his best for last, when in the span of a single evening he showed all three types of impulsive behavior we have seen in this section. First, he fell asleep while Jesus prayed in Gethsemane, causing the Lord to comment on his weak willpower. Then he turned into an explosive short fuse and cut off Malchus' ear. Finally, he became an impulsive liar when he was asked three times if he was one of Jesus' friends. Peter was headstrong and impulsive by nature, but God was able to transform his character from within through his commitment to the Lord Jesus Christ.

New Ways of Relating to These People

COMPULSIVE STYLES

1. Approach these people in a casual, carefree, and playful spirit. Be a person without guile.
2. Refocus their sense of duty on their "obligation" to spend time playing and relaxing with their family and friends.
3. For those who cannot seem to sit still, show them how to channel their energies into more constructive and rewarding activities.
4. Suggest they read Wayne Oates's book *Workaholics: Make Laziness Work for You* (Doubleday & Co., 1978).
5. Teach loved ones how to relax the pressure by lowering their expectations of the compulsive person. They do not have to earn God's love. Why *earn* anyone else's love?
6. For compulsives who are Christians, explore what Jesus meant in his words to Mary and Martha in Luke 10. Remind them of the fourth commandment, which sanctifies rest as a religious duty. Encourage them to read Isaiah 40.

IMPULSIVE STYLES

1. Approach them with cautious foresight. Enjoy their spontaneity, but be ever mindful of the dangers in situations that tempt them.
2. Encourage them to avoid temptation by changing the situations they live in, and by praying the Lord's Prayer when tempted.
3. Within an otherwise supportive relationship, react quickly and negatively when they offend you. Don't let the sun go down on your anger.
4. With impulsive liars, temporarily restrict your trust of them, and if necessary, their privileges.
5. With overcautious dropouts, make it uncomfortable for them to hide in a corner from people. Be ready to offer encouragement and direct assistance when they seek involvement again.

6. Styles of Relating to Others

This chapter is about people who can't seem to find a healthy balance in their relationships with others. Some of them want to be too closely dependent on another person. The following section on Dependent Styles describes several not-so-successful ways of handling strong needs for a safe, close relationship. Some people have had these needs frustrated by being rejected at an early age. Many of these have reacted by trying to strangle their need to depend on another person. They seem unable to get close to anyone. Instead, they acquire the things they need for security (money, sex, companionship, etc.). *People* are then used in order to get *things.* Some of their styles of using others to meet their needs are described in the second section, Manipulative Styles.

DEPENDENT STYLES

"How can you stand there and watch me suffer?"

The dependent character style is the most common one of all. Children are naturally dependent on their parents in early years, and some people never do work through that primary attachment. Parents sometimes encourage this dependency. For example, they can cause their children to doubt their own judgment, self-control, abilities, and self-worth. Or they can teach their children to mistrust all others outside the home, and to believe that no one will ever be able to take better care of them than mom and dad. These helpless children usually run away from home, going from the frying pan into the fire. They run off and marry someone without ever learning the inner security that comes only from living alone. They trade in their apron strings for an equally clinging dependency on their new spouse.

Dependent people usually cannot grow into emotional maturity without first depending on someone who believes in their own growing inner strength. One excellent way to express this belief in other people's potential is to let them struggle through a crisis without rescuing them. Stand beside and behind them, cheering them on. For in the end they must be able to look back and recognize the strength and ability they found within themselves. There will always be a few birds who would never learn to fly if it weren't for the wise, courageous mother who knows when they need to be pushed out of the nest.

The Emotional Cripple. The most common examples of a dependent personality are what I call emotional cripples. They can't endure the emotional pains of living without leaning on another person to support them like a crutch. A physically disabled person who neglects to exercise the weak parts of the body will become more and more disabled. Emotional cripples have not exercised their abilities to solve problems, tolerate frustrations, and take care of themselves. You want to tell these people to stand up for themselves, but they would rather have you do it for them.

These people are known for their desperate pleas for help when they are threatened. Their greatest fear is that of being abandoned by the person to whom they have become attached. When they become insecure, they counter with a threat of their own, to fall apart emotionally. If you don't rescue them, their pleas (or threats) become more and more desperate. "I would feel lost without you." "I couldn't stand the loneliness." "I have this weird sense that we were meant to be together." "I would be helpless." "I feel like I'm losing my mind." "Life isn't worth living." "I want to kill myself. I will. Tonight." And if necessary, the final hooker, "It'll be on your conscience." As a final kick in the teeth, they want to leave us their misery in their will.

There comes a time when you realize you don't want to bail them out again. You wonder, if you don't, who will? And if no one does, can they make it? At this point, you realize that your resentment of their drain on you has begun to poison the love you once had for them. It can only get worse until they start to grow up.

You can back out in three ways. If you really believe they can make it, go cold turkey. Tell them you think they can do it themselves, and *should* for their own self-respect. Or you can give them partial support and expect them to do the rest on their own. A third suggestion is to encourage them to start depending on someone else, someone who believes in his own inner strength. It could be a friend, a counselor, a pastor, or a church. In any case, make it plain that their becoming more self-reliant will not end your relationship with them. Rather, it will make it closer and more comfortable.

The Crisis Creator. In one variation of the emotional cripple, some people pull the dependency strings by creating a crisis, or by subtly allowing one to happen. Crisis creators may see the connection between the latest crisis and their continuing panic over dependency. "Mother is real sick, and I just need somebody to be with me tonight." "Oh, my car is broken down (wrecked, etc.). Won't you stay with me until it is fixed?" More often, the crisis is a health break-down, like the big heart attack Fred Sanford would feel coming on when his son talked about leaving. One woman I saw filed suit three times to divorce her husband. Each time he checked into a hospital with cardiac problems, but all tests turned out to be negative. Each time, she dropped the petition for divorce.

These people really put you in a bind. About the only thing you can do is tell them that the next time, they will need to make alternate plans for a white knight to rescue them from their distress. You help them make the plan, but you must remind them that these crises are draining away your concern for them. You are offering them a more mature, *mutually* supportive friendship, one that will be more enjoyable for you both.

The Doormat. Here lie the hearts and souls of people we call henpecked husbands and overly submissive wives. They are suffering servants to a fault, second-class citizens in their own homes. A colleague once told me, "I never saw a doormat who didn't like to do a little stompin' once in a while." I believe that, and I believe in the Christian model of submis-siveness for *both* husband and wife. I am talking about help-less, immature people, who maintain their dependency by always accommodating their needs to the wants, wishes, and whims of someone else.

I can remember the first year of our marriage. One of us would ask, "What do you want, honey?" "Oh, I don't care, whatever you want, dear," the other would reply. "No, precious, you decide." I remember one time standing like that for almost a minute trying to choose where we would sit at a movie. That much submission chokes the growing life out of a relationship.

More often you see one person who has chosen to take the doormat role. For those who live with a doormat, your mates are probably afraid of losing you if they express one of their desires or needs. To bring them out of it, it's not enough to invite them to express what they want (this is usually too frightening). You must prove that your needs don't count as much as theirs, by just *waiting* for them to tell you what they need. Don't lose patience and start doing what *you* need. They need to know that you care enough to sit with them and share the frustration of their not knowing their needs, or of their being too afraid to express them.

If you are one of the doormats, hitch up your pants and look at your mate eyeball to eyeball. Say that you feel stepped on, and are either too afraid, or by now too out of touch with yourself, to stand up and ask for what you need. Tell how you know it is making you a miserable person to live with, and ask if your mate would like to see you grow up and become a more equal partner in the relationship. If the answer is no, I hope you can and will assert that you will grow up, with or without assistance. You *can* do it, and it's the best thing you can do for you both.

The Ego Smasher. Unfortunately, many cripples, crisis creators, and especially doormats have attached themselves to ego smashers. Ego smashers are also insecure and dependent, but they hide these feelings. They see all their own helplessness in their mates. They come across as the dominating, macho husband, or the emasculating, henpecking wife. They think they have it all together, that they could make it just fine on their own. They continually put down their mates, calling them helpless, worthless, unfaithful, dishonest, selfish, ignorant, lazy, evil, low-down, and no good. But their dependency shows, because it is precisely when their mates start showing some independence and self-respect that ego smashers get threatened. Then they begin to sense their own insecurity, because they are losing their hold over their mates. If they can't browbeat them into meeting their needs (especially the need for ego boosters), then they are faced with their own feelings of helplessness and worthlessness. As long as their mates will digest it, they will dish out the criticism that says, "I may be no good, but I'm better than you."

The natural response to such an attack is to throw it back in their faces, or to stand back and say, "No I'm not, and I'm not going to sit and listen to it anymore." Neither of these defensive reactions is likely to help your relationship. Try waving a white towel or flashing the peace sign. Then invite them to bury the hatchet and join you in trying to be more supportive of each other. If they don't go for this, believe it or not, you are the stronger of the two. It's you who need to support your mate. If you can't do it, get yourself enough support outside the relationship where you can start being the peacemaker and comforter in your home. Chances are when you can do this, sooner or later your mate will reciprocate.

MANIPULATIVE STYLES

"Yes, but what will he do for me?"

The dependent characters previously discussed are wanting to be too closely dependent on other persons. Those with manipulative styles have the opposite problem. They don't want to get close to anybody. They are deeply afraid to depend on anyone, for fear of being hurt or rejected. While dependent people usually come from parents who wanted to be too close to their children, manipulators usually come from emotionally rejecting parents. They knew so little warmth and affection while they were growing up that they have given up on finding love. They have convinced themselves that they don't need close companionship. They have pulled back from *people* and sought comfort in *things* they can acquire and hold on to for security. They are seeking things like money, fame, power, success, and pleasure. They think people are only as good as what you can get from them.

Manipulators seem to be detached from other people, even though they spend plenty of time with others and seem to be self-confident and secure. They are usually unable to empathize with the feelings of other people, so they feel very little shame or guilt. They are often charming and easy to be with, but they use this facade to deceive and influence others.

Of all the character styles discussed in this book, people with manipulative styles are probably the most difficult to change. They would rather do without your company than to change their ways. They seldom experience much emotional suffering, and so they aren't motivated to change. Their security is derived from things, which they often learn to manipulate fairly well. How we change as people has little effect on them. Dealing with these people is very difficult indeed. Successful efforts to change their personalities have been few and far between. Often the best thing you can do is to revise what you expect of them, and get out of any position that requires you to depend on them.

Narcissus. In Greek mythology, Narcissus was the young man who fell in love with his own reflection in the water. He spent his life in frustration, seeking a closer relationship with this beautiful person who looked up at him from the water. American psychologists have become so successful at preaching the virtues of self-analysis that this decade has often been called "the age of narcissism." It's "hip" to explore the depths of your psyche, but it's easy to lose relationships with others in the process.

People with a narcissistic character disorder are described as craving the admiration of others. They impress you as charming, superficial, gregarious, self-confident, and unable to feel guilt or empathize with others. They tend to hang around others for attention and praise, using them in subtle ways to make themselves look good. Spiritually, theirs is the chief of the seven deadly sins—pride. They see no need for God or other people, because they have elevated their self-esteem one notch above everyone else.

Examples of narcissism abound in America today. These people we say are "stuck on themselves." Two excellent examples are the characters described in the songs "Big Shot," by Billy Joel, and "You're So Vain," by Carly Simon. I once knew a man who kissed himself in the mirror each morning after he shaved, and he lived his whole life as if he were on stage. But the Narcissus I know best is myself. My wife and friends agree with me that what most alienates me from others is my vanity. I tend to rationalize away all my guilt, fear, and anger. I try to impress others by acting as if I'm a super-Christian, a superpsychologist, a superathlete, or a superhusband.

We all have an image or mask that we like to show the world. Sometimes we get caught up in playing the role and begin to believe we *are* the mask. Narcissists not only identify with their image, they fall in love with it. I would probably still be in love with my mask if two things had not happened to me at nearly the same time. First, my wife, Molly, had begun to see the lonely little boy behind the mask, and she was able to love me as I really was. Secondly, I lost all my admirers when I went from being a big shot at a little high school to a nobody at college. I was lucky enough to fall out of love with my mask and to fall in love with Molly before I could get another act together.

So for those who try to relate to people who are stuck on themselves, there are two ways you can go. The easiest and safest road is to change yourself, so that you see and relate to the people behind the mask who are trying to impress you. Once you can look underneath the charm, are you still attracted? Tell them about it. Give them a chance to come out from behind the mask when they are with you.

Even if you do care about the person behind the role, narcissists aren't likely to give up on their image until everybody else stops admiring them for it. Pride doesn't often go away until after a fall. So your other approach can be to debunk the character's admiring audience. Most inflated egos are going to need both approaches in order to change—the one-two punch of others' total rejection of their mask, and someone's solid acceptance of the person behind the mask.

The Organization Man. Of all the masks people wear to gain approval, "the corporate image" has become famous for the way it can swallow up a person's self-concept and undermine personal relationships. Social climbers come in all shapes and sizes, but some business executives seem to stand out in any crowd. These people put job promotions as their top priority, over family, religion, and health. They all show the same corporate appearance, social life, political views, leisure activities, and even personal tastes in music and art. One man seems to do everything with his business interests in mind. The sole reason he married was that a promotion depended on it; and he pretends to enjoy making love to his wife so that she'll pretend to adore him when they are in public.

Not all corporate types are executives with a black briefcase and a gray three-piece suit. Any big organization has its share, including federal and state governments. Charles Colson's book, *Born Again,* describes how he began to lose his identity in working under the Nixon Administration. In big politics, people are used and deceived to meet needs of the organization that become more important than any personal needs. One of the favorite ways these people have of manipulating others is "hiding behind the office." In this game, people pretend that they have no personal feelings. They say that their every action is dictated by the all-important demands of their lofty position. Richard Nixon used to refer to himself as "the President" so often that I wondered if even he forgot who he was underneath the Presidential role.

Dealing with these people opens new vistas for the old adage, "If you can't beat 'em, join 'em." This has been the only answer for many a corporate "widow." These neglected spouses content themselves with playing second fiddle, waiting for the inevitable time when hubby's corporate star begins to fall. They figure the more they give to their spouses' careers now, the more they will be loved and cared for when retirement comes. These practical people have faced the facts. Other wives of organization men have challenged for top billing while their husband's star was still on the rise. The overwhelming majority of these women either give up, or their marriages end in divorce.

The Career Criminal (alias the Antisocial Personality). Whereas Narcissus wanted everyone's attention and approval, the organization man chooses to seek acceptance primarily through one certain group in society. The career criminal takes this one step further—he doesn't need a response from anybody. People diagnosed as "antisocial personality" have set themselves against the rest of the human race. They are looking out for Number One, and nobody else. They show little or no loyalty to any code of conduct, social group, or personal friend. They seek their own pleasure at others' expense, showing no sense of responsibility or concern for others' feelings. They are often able to disguise their dishonesty through charm and cleverness. Repeated shame and punishment do not seem to faze them. They seem forever unable or unwilling to change their basically selfish, criminal, and pleasure-oriented life-styles.

If people take up the criminal life-style early, they will turn out to be rough characters who keep getting into trouble with the law. They spend much of their youth on the street or in institutions. I knew quite a few persons of this type during my three years working in a state institution for disturbed children and adolescents. We had children there as young as seven who showed no desire to relate closely to any of the staff or other children. They wanted their own pleasure above all, and right now if not sooner.

One twelve-year-old boy was so hardhearted I couldn't believe it. His consuming passion in life was to get as much of everything—cigarettes, money, and above all, freedom— as he could get. All his various emotional outbursts were understood in the light of those goals. I offered him a personal friendship several times each week for over a year. The longer I worked with him, the more determined he became to push me away. He acted out all his impulses to break things, hurt people, steal, kiss women, tell lies, run away, and hurt himself. He would express no guilt or regret for any of these actions. The only personal help he would let me give him was teaching him how to manipulate others more cleverly. As with so many children who *act* disturbed to avoid a locked institution, we finally sent him to a correctional facility.

Some people give up on trusting others later in life, during adolescence or adulthood. If these people have some intelligence and a respectable family background, they are likely to become successful as white-collar criminals. This variety of antisocial personality is smoother and more polished than their street-grown, "hard core" criminal cousins. But they can be just as tough as anybody at the core. Sometimes people evolve into this profession through fear of failure at playing the organization man. All these people are driven by the consuming thirst to acquire things through using people.

So what does it take to change these selfish, ruthless, impulsive, hardhearted souls? The clearest examples of permanent change in such people have been through religious conversion experiences. Although prayer and forgiving love are common ingredients, there is no set formula for converting the career criminal.

The next best hope, and usually the first step to take, is to stop covering for these people. Let them face the music and serve the full penalty of the civil law. The ideal institution for such people has the following characteristics. It has the physical limits and personal supervision to restrict opportunities for acting out selfish impulses. It provides socially positive individuals and groups whom they can identify with and imitate. It teaches acceptable social conduct by example, instruction, and restriction of privileges to punish violations of the social code. Finally, it offers support for all of their basic human needs.

But such institutions are rare. Available tax money gets lost in bureaucratic black holes and face-saving programs for this or that taxpayer. If you are one of those having to live with career criminals, take this advice: Don't hang yourself on a cross that bears the inscription "One-Man Reform Movement." Your best bet is to keep from being used, and love from a distance. Pray for God to break their hard hearts through his discipline and love. Once the Lord has broken the heart, a sweet spirit of genuine repentance comes flowing out. *Then* you can be there to express your forgiveness, and to welcome them back into God's family.

New Ways of Relating to These People

DEPENDENT STYLES

1. Approach these people supportively, but only when they are trying to help themselves or someone else. When they are feeling sorry for themselves, give advice and pull back until they follow it.
2. When you begin to feel drained by one of their crises, back off and let them learn some new solutions to their problems. Let them learn to bear their own burdens.
3. Between crises, help them make more mature, responsible "disaster plans" for the next emergency.
4. With overly accommodating doormats, force them into expressing what *they* want once in a while, and go along with them if possible.
5. With overly critical ego smashers, get more support for yourself outside your relationships with them. You cannot bear this burden alone. Then you can start building *them* up without letting them put you down in the process.

MANIPULATIVE STYLES

1. Approach these people with wise, skeptical caution, asking yourself how they might be able to take advantage of you.
2. Keep your romantic and savioristic love for them on your end of a ten-foot pole.
3. Remember that they are more concerned with *things* than with people's feelings.
4. With ego trippers who are enamored with their self-images, try to ignore the facade and relate to the insecure person behind the mask.

5. If you are married to an "organization man," tough it out for a while. The more you support him now, the more he'll love you later.

6. With criminal characters, wait for society's punishment and discipline to break their hearts. Only then can they share committed love.

7. Don't try to protect these people from legal or financial disaster—it is often the very medicine they need to cure them of manipulating people.

7. Love Seasoned with Wisdom

Can it be that showing your love for someone could do more harm than good? It often seems that way when you love persons with a character disorder. The more you try to take care of them, or fall in love with them, the more your expressions of love seem to poison the relationship. Jesus seemed to recognize that with certain people, showing Christian love can do more harm than good to you both. "Do not throw your pearls before swine, lest they trample them under foot and turn to attack you" (Mt. 7:6). Your love gets crushed by the hurt, and when your love is gone, you get attacked yourself!

Jesus sent his disciples out into the world by warning them, "Behold, I send you out as sheep in the midst of wolves; so be wise as serpents and innocent as doves" (Mt. 10:16). Wisdom is needed to focus your love where it will do the most good. If your expression of love for someone is to be received, both of you must know who you're loving. This chapter deals with understanding people more fully, so that your love will not be trampled underfoot.

There is one particular view of humankind that I find most consistent with my training in psychology, my common sense, and my Christian faith. I see people experiencing life in four dimensions—body, heart, mind, and soul. We sense our physical needs (impulses) through the body, our emotional needs (feelings) through the heart, our intellectual needs (thoughts) through the mind, and our spiritual needs for life itself through the soul. The way we choose to focus our awareness on these needs is the free choice we have as human beings. The more we pay attention to any one need, the stronger it becomes. Being dominated by an attitude, habit, or emotion prevents the full experience of Christ's life in us.

God created the soul as the dwelling place for his spirit, to harmonize the body, heart, and mind toward doing his will. When the human will habitually pays more attention to one of the lower aspects of experience, the harmony between our needs is lost. One style of acting, thinking, or feeling begins to dominate the personality. People who want to form a close relationship are put off and hurt. So, in personal relationships as well as in the experience of competing needs, the person suffers from a character disorder.

When you show love for such a disordered character, whom are you loving? Character styles become masks that hide the living soul God created. For example, suppose you show love to a man dominated by an obsessive style of thinking. He will tend to believe that you are loving his devotion to duty, for that is how he sees himself at the core. No, you are loving the person behind the pressure. That person just happens to hassle himself continually. Now and then you invite him to get himself together, and love someone with all his body, mind, heart, and soul. That is the way God wants us to love him (Mk. 12:29–30).

What kind of love should you show to these people? Not the sentimental, gushy kind of love that seeks to take care of them or save them—that is your Achilles' heel. Your expressions of concern must be what nursing schools are now calling "tough loving care." This kind of love cannot be killed with hurt. The Greek word the Bible uses for it is *agapē*. This love is a gift from God that demands nothing in return. It is described in all its glory in 1 Corinthians 13. Sharing this love has two unusual effects. The more of it you give away, the more of it you have. And instead of spoiling people, it has the power to transform them into the image of Christ.

One danger in dealing with persons with character disorders is the tendency to look down on them. It is easy to find yourself playing God and judging their behavior as absolutely right or absolutely wrong. I have done this in the past, but I have learned to ask myself, "How can you be sure you wouldn't have sinned even greater if you had been born into his skin?" And how can I be sure what alternatives he could think of, whether he might not have chosen the lesser of two evils? The Bible asks us several more questions to keep us from judging. Might you have once done the same sort of thing yourself, or taught him this behavior by your example? (See Jn. 8:7.) Are you now tempted to do the same thing he is doing? (See Gal. 6:1.) Have you dealt with this problem fully enough so that it doesn't cloud your vision of the other person? (See Mt. 7:4, 5.)

Once you quit judging, you *can* comment on the *wisdom* of their behavior in reference to their own stated goals. In this way, you are not relating as their judge or critic, but rather as a friend trying to help them reach their goal.

A great deal of what I have said in this book about relating to character disorders is expressed strongly in these two verses of Scripture:

> And the Lord's servant must not be quarrelsome but kindly to every one, an apt teacher, forbearing, correcting his opponents with gentleness. God may perhaps grant that they will repent and come to know the truth. 2 Tim. 2:24, 25

This passage reminds us of several things. Don't struggle against them—you'll both lose. Be kind and patient—use wise *agapē*. Teach them how they are frustrating themselves. Gently correct their offenses to you, so that you don't become put out or worn out with them. Finally, don't forget that God (not you) may (and may not) grant that they (not you again) will repent (a complete character change), and come to know the truth (to see God, themselves, and others as they really are).

Finally, I invite you to adapt this prayer, which I have used in my own efforts to cope with a difficult man:

> Our Father, you know how much I have struggled and suffered, trying to love this person I bring to you now. I confess that I can neither change his heart nor produce any more love for him in my own heart. Sometimes it seems that I don't even know him. To cleanse my soul of resentment, I forgive him now of any wrongs which he has done. Forgive me also for the ignorant and sometimes selfish mistakes I have made with him

in the past. Through the discipline and the comfort of your love, help him to break down the walls he hides behind. Reassure him of your tender care and forgiveness, that he may come to know you as his Savior and Lord.

Grant unto me now your wisdom to know what *he* needs from me most of all. Fill my heart with your tough loving care, that I may seek to meet these needs while trusting you to meet my own. I am grateful for the many people who bring me your blessings, and for your abiding spirit of love in our souls. I trust that all this will unfold to your honor and glory. Amen.

References

Backus, D. "The Seven Deadly Sins: Their Meaning and Measurement." Doctoral dissertation, University of Minnesota, 1969. Published on demand by Xerox University Microfilms, Ann Arbor, Michigan.

Berne, Eric *Games People Play*. Ballantine Books, 1964.

Cleckley, H. M. *The Mask of Sanity*, 4th ed. C. V. Mosby, 1964.

Colson, Charles. *Born Again*. Fleming H. Revell Co., 1976.

Erikson, Erik. *Childhood and Society*. W. W. Norton & Co., 1950.

———. *Insight and Responsibility*. W. W. Norton & Co., 1964.

Fairlee, Henry. *The Seven Deadly Sins Today*. New Republic Books, 1978.

Glasser, William. *Reality Therapy*. Harper & Row, 1965.

Kohlberg, Lawrence. "Moral Stages and Moralization: The Cognitive-Developmental Approach." In Thomas Lickona (ed.), *Moral Development and Behavior*. Holt, Rinehart & Winston, 1976.

Menninger, Karl. *Whatever Became of Sin?* Hawthorn Books, 1973.

Oates, Wayne. *On Becoming Children of God*. Westminster Press, 1968.

———. *Workaholics: Make Laziness Work for You*. Doubleday & Co., 1978.

Perls, Frederick. S. *In and Out of the Garbage Pail*. Real People Press, 1969.

Piaget, Jean. *The Moral Judgment of the Child*. Harcourt and Brace, 1932.

Reich, Wilhelm. *Character Analysis*, 3d ed. Noonday Press, 1949.

Schmidt, P. The Character Assessment Scale: A New Tool for the Counselor," *Pastoral Psychology*, in press.

Schmidt, P.; Oates, W.; and Backus, D. "The Sinful Attitudes Inventory: A Manual for Administration, Scoring, and Follow-up Counseling." Unpublished manuscript, 1977.

Shapiro, David. *Neurotic Styles.* Basic Books, 1965.

Sherrill, Lewis J. *The Struggle of the Soul.* Macmillan Co., 1951.

Szasz, Thomas. *The Myth of Mental Illness.* Rev. ed. Harper & Row, 1974.

———. *The Myth of Psychotherapy.* Harper & Row, 1978.